The

SAINT-DOMINGUE
PLANTATION

The

SAINT-DOMINGUE PLANTATION;

or,

THE INSURRECTION

A DRAMA IN FIVE ACTS

CHARLES DE RÉMUSAT

Translated by NORMAN R. SHAPIRO
With an Introduction and Notes by DORIS Y. KADISH

LOUISIANA STATE UNIVERSITY PRESS BATON ROUGE

Published by Louisiana State University Press
Copyright © 2008 by Louisiana State University Press
An LSU Press Paperback Original
Manufactured in the United States of America
First printing

Designer: Barbara Neely Bourgoyne
Typefaces: Century, display; Century Old Style, text
Printer and binder: Thomson-Shore, Inc.

Library of Congress Cataloging-in-Publication Data
Rémusat, Charles de, 1797–1875.
  [Habitation de Saint-Domingue, ou, L'insurrection. English]
  The Saint-Domingue plantation, or, The insurrection : a drama in five acts /
Charles de Rémusat ; translated by Norman R. Shapiro ; with an introduction and
notes by Doris Y. Kadish.
    p. cm.
  ISBN 978-0-8071-3357-6 (pbk. : alk. paper) 1. Haiti—History—Revolution,
1791–1804—Drama. I. Shapiro, Norman R. II. Kadish, Doris Y. III. Title. IV. Title:
Saint-Domingue plantation. V. Title: Insurrection.
  PQ2386.R36H3213 2008
  842'.7—dc22
                                                                2008023380

Publication of this play has been supported by a grant to the translator
from the Thomas and Catharine McMahon Fund of Wesleyan University,
established through the generosity of the late Joseph McMahon.

The paper in this book meets the guidelines for permanence and
durability of the Committee on Production Guidelines for Book Longevity
of the Council on Library Resources. ∞

CONTENTS

Map of Saint-Domingue appears opposite page 1.

TRANSLATOR'S NOTE

Theater, like poetry, presents the translator with more of an artistic challenge than fiction. Although I believe firmly that all literature, ideally, is meant to be heard, even if only in the head, fiction writers (and hence their translators) are, by the very nature of the genre, generally less concerned with matters of sound and tonal nuance than their dramatic and poetic colleagues. Which is not to say that they ought not be. Translating the likes of an eighteenth-century French novel into contemporary American idiom, for example (except as an intentional pastiche or burlesque), would be unthinkable. It might purport to be an adaptation, but not a translation in the true sense of the word.

Still, if fiction translators can (and, I think, should) choose to write "with an eye toward the ear," verse and theater translators haven't the luxury of choice. Those who take their craft seriously will, I think, feel obliged to do so. Even the most abstruse poet expects a living reciter/listener out there somewhere; although, perhaps, one who may have to stop, repeat several times, and ponder on the text before really "getting it," whether the "it" is in the original or filtered through a translation. With drama the author has even less of a choice. Plays are written to be performed, not merely contemplated on paper. When read, even in silence, they are no less performed in the mind of the reader, who also has the option, lacking in a stage performance, of stopping for reflection

and jumping forward or back at will, from scene to scene. What's
more, the translator of theater has the further obligation to trans-
mit not only the "meaning" of the text, whether the "performance"
is virtual or real, inside the head or out, but also—pardon the tru-
ism—its tone.

Charles de Rémusat's *L'Habitation de Saint-Domingue; ou,
L'Insurrection* is a case in point. It was never actually staged (although read from time to time in contemporary artistic salons),
but its very existence as a play implies, ipso facto, that its author
certainly hoped—expected?—that it would be performed at some
time, and no doubt wrote it with spectators in mind. Striking
though it is as a vehicle for his timely social and philosophical ide-
ology, as theater it should not be relegated to the status of a mere
archival document. But it would be clear, I think, to anyone reading the original, and especially to one setting about to translate it,
that, for all its powerful dramatic action, its theatricality must have
been less a concern to Rémusat than its ideological intent and its
pertinent contemporary message.

As a result, one of the difficulties in effectively translating the
play lay precisely in Rémusat's seemingly rather casual attitude
toward nuts-and-bolts matters of stagecraft. For him, so long as
his message rang out loud and clear, any shortcomings in dramatic technique could, it appears, be overlooked. Are his stage
settings and directions, unlike those of his typical French Romantic contemporaries, rather vague? Is too much left to the reader's
imagination and dramatic intuition? Do entrances and exits remain
a little too imprecise? Are characters free to position themselves
more or less at their own (or a director's) will? What do they all
do while such-and-such a character is delivering a lengthy tirade
or dialoguing with others? And is it realistic for such often lengthy
speeches, however packed with philosophical and social specula-
tion, to plow forward uninterrupted, unrelieved by an interlocu-
tor's "oh" or "ah," or by another character's well-motivated reflec-
tions? Rémusat appears little taken with such practical concerns

for the ideal of theatrical *vraisemblance*. Nor does he seem overly bothered by details, such that two characters in chains in one act appear bound by rope in the next, or even such that a character unmentioned in the *dramatis personae* suddenly appears in the action to deliver a single line. But such "flaws" are unimportant when the overall strengths of the play—its message and its dramatic development and illustration—remain powerfully intact...

A translator faced with such arguably secondary theatrical shortcomings has to decide whether to remain rigorously faithful to the original with its occasional blemishes, or to smooth them out for the sake of consistency, though without altering to any significant degree the basic text: its plot, its dialogue, its compelling *coups de théâtre*. My own choice, as with all my theater translations, comic as well as serious, has been to follow the second course in a modest effort to make the play more stageworthy in its décor, directions, and such externals; and to do so while intentionally retaining a "period" tone in the English dialogue corresponding to that of the French, and by respecting its characters' varying nuances of pomposity, idealism, religiosity, terror, and eventually utter despair... And even its moments of restrained humor. My aim, as always, has been to retain the undeniable literary and philosophical strengths of the play and, at the same time, to make it more readily actable without wrenching it from its original context. Like a doctor observing the Hippocratic oath, I have tried, while performing the surgery of translation, "above all, to do no harm..."

I hope that this spectacular drama may eventually have the stage performances it deserves, albeit transposed into a language that its author did not intend, but one whose fidelity to both meaning and tone I would hope he might find fitting.

INTRODUCTION

DORIS Y. KADISH

Time has nearly obliterated the memory of one of the most notable literary and political figures of the first half of the nineteenth century, Charles François Marie, comte de Rémusat (1797–1875). That is not to say that his name does not appear in the historical record under a number of different guises: as a leading force in the opposition to the Restoration government in the 1820s and, again, to the Second Empire in 1851; as an elected member of the Chambre des députés from 1830 to 1848; as an inductee into the Académie française in 1846; as minister of foreign affairs in 1871 and deputy again in 1873. Indeed, Rémusat stands center stage for many of the most important events of French nineteenth-century political life: "Chief editor of the *Globe*, he joined Thiers in writing the famous manifesto of liberal newspapers against the *ordonnances* of Charles X. Minister of the interior, he had Louis Bonaparte arrested in Boulogne pretending to restore the Empire . . . He was at the Tuileries, behind Louis-Philippe . . . when the king signed his abdication" (Arlet xxii–xxiv).

Although clearly all the phases of Rémusat's life merit consideration, it is the period of the 1820s that has the greatest literary importance and perhaps the greatest historical importance as well.

As Darío Roldán writes, during this period, "everything was being rethought: the concepts of sovereignty, representation, the role of the chambers, the principles of legitimate monarchy, the foundations of obedience, etc." (Roldán 38). During this decade Rémusat played a crucial oppositional role vis-à-vis the forces of reaction in society and came to personify his generation's views on constitutional monarchy, electoral reforms, freedom of the press, and other liberal political issues. It was also in the 1820s, after a hiatus of more than two decades following the revolutions in Haiti, that the French antislavery movement was reborn. Through his published writings in *Le Globe,* his dramatic readings in French salons, and his participation in the creation of the Société de la morale chrétienne, Rémusat contributed to that rebirth. Moreover, the 1820s saw the birth of Romanticism in France, following the earlier incarnations of that movement in Germany and Britain. Although Rémusat was not a major Romantic writer, he was one of the first and the most influential to articulate the principles of the new movement and the cultural transformation it represented. And although not published at the time, his small body of theatrical works from the 1820s—*Jean de Montciel, ou Le Fief; La Saint-Barthélemy; L'Habitation de Saint-Domingue, ou L'Insurrection*—represents the style and the spirit of the new movement.

The period of the 1820s also has considerable importance with respect to colonial history. After several years of negotiations, it was finally in 1825 that Charles X recognized the independence of Haiti, an act that opened the door for recognition by other countries loath to incur the displeasure of France. Although the price that Haiti paid for the acknowledgment of its legitimacy as a nation was exorbitant reparations earmarked to repay former colonists for their lost property, French moderates and even most former colonists saw Charles X's act as a humanitarian gesture that would make Haiti a symbol of hope for oppressed people worldwide and a first step in bringing about the end of the illegal slave trade and the inhuman treatment of slaves in the remaining French colonies.

In contrast, conservatives saw the act as a betrayal of the former colonists, a recognition of the black insurrection, and an abandonment of part of the French kingdom.

On a variety of levels, then, Rémusat's role in the 1820s merits reconsideration today. It provides a window onto his contribution to literary history as well as, more generally, onto the development of French social and political ideas in the nineteenth century. The many sides of his literary, political, and historical thought are especially evident in his antislavery play *L'Habitation de Saint-Domingue.* Never performed, the play was first read in the salon of Paul Dubois, the editor of *Le Globe,* on February 22, 1825; subsequent readings occurred in the salons of Mme de Broglie and Mme de Catelan (Riegert 127). To understand the play and its significance, it is necessary to consider the context in which it was written, its central conflict, and the abolitionist implications of its multiple main characters.

Charles de Rémusat epitomizes the complex, transitional world of early-nineteenth-century France. Although he was exposed from a young age to the charms and graces of the *ancien régime*—"for the young Rémusat, the salon preceded school" (Sainte-Beuve 917)—post-revolutionary aristocratic society was far less politically cohesive than in the earlier era. His own family displayed the fissures and discordances of the society to which they belonged. Whereas Rémusat's father was strictly anticlerical and his maternal grandmother, Adélaïde de Vergennes, embodied the liberal, Voltairian spirit of the eighteenth century, his mother leaned toward the values of legitimate monarchy and religion (Ozouf 157). What is more, his parents played important social and political roles during the Napoleonic as well as the Restoration governments. Thus, from the start, Rémusat learned to reconcile competing political philosophies and to adapt to the conditions of a society in constant flux. Indeed, Honoré de Balzac is said to have chosen Rémusat as the model for his charming, chameleonlike character Henri de Marsay, the ultimate social hybrid (Kadish, "Hybrids" 270–78). Like the young Rémusat of the 1820s, de Marsay personifies the conjunction of old and new, empire and monarchy, remembrance and erasure of the legacy of the French Revolution. Rémusat did not actually have an English father as does his fictional avatar, de Marsay. But the intellectual trends that held sway among liberals during his lifetime derived in large measure from Britain: Romanticism, constitutional monarchy, abolitionism, and many of the related intellectual currents that conservatives of the time such as Balzac deplored. As Pierre Rosanvallon states, "Charles de Rémusat is probably the author who best tried to think through the relationship between English and French political culture in the nineteenth century" (Roldán iii).

Certain political tendencies from the 1820s remained more or less constant throughout Rémusat's intellectual and political life, however. He belonged to the group of progressive intellectuals known at the time as "Doctrinaires" and, for a time, to that of more leftist liberals as well. As with others who ultimately came to support the Orléanist cause, he wanted a government that was both monarchical (a single figure of authority) and republican (legal equality and freedom of the press); and he saw the Charter of 1830 as the basis in France of the kind of constitutional monarchy he admired in Britain. He retained a lifelong belief in the salutary effect of the French Revolution: if not in all of its consequences, at least in its intent to create a free society. The increased influence of reactionary "ultras" and the Bourbon monarchy's shift to the political right after 1820 affirmed his faith in the goals of the French Revolution. Yet he states that he never felt bitterness toward the Restoration: "In a sense I was grateful to it for having given me the ideas that I used against it" (Sainte-Beuve 923). Near the end of his life, in 1873, he summarized the political beliefs that had sustained his long and varied career: "All that I ever wanted was the regular and peaceful victory of the great principles of the French

Revolution. That is what I wanted from monarchy, and that is what I want today from the Republic, which I hope to see maintained with resolution and organized with wisdom" (Roldán 27).

Rémusat's faith in the legacy of the French Revolution, which is central to an understanding of *L'Habitation de Saint-Domingue,* dates back to his reading of Germaine de Staël's *Considérations sur la révolution française,* published after her death in 1817. At that time, frank assessments or even detailed information about the revolution was not readily available. Rémusat's response to Staël's book, which appeared under the title "De l'influence du dernier ouvrage de Madame de Staël sur la jeune opinion publique," was prefaced by François Guizot and published in the *Archives philosophiques, politiques, et littéraires* in 1818. Reactions to the article and its open condemnation of Napoleon were strong. Staël's influential children—Auguste de Staël and Albertine de Broglie—welcomed Rémusat into their circle. Not only did the political views he expressed conform to theirs, their mother's, and those of her Groupe de Coppet. They and others were pleasantly surprised to see that the son of parents who had served in the imperial government dared to denounce Napoleon, who had exiled Staël from France following the publication of her novel *Delphine* in 1802. In contrast to the liberal reaction to the article, Rémusat's mother responded with consternation. In a letter to her husband she wrote: "Charles's article is at once both pleasing and highly unpleasant. In general it gives a good idea of his intelligence. But it is shocking to ultras. For our social group it seems to be a useless and overly blunt display of his opinions. And, to make matters worse, the liberals rave about it. If you want to know what I really think, I am angry that he published it, and I cannot forgive myself for having encouraged him to do so" (Roldán 36). Twenty years later, Rémusat himself chose to remove the part about Napoleon altogether when he republished the article in his essay collection *Passé et présent* (Roldán 47).

In agreement with Staël, who is only actually mentioned at the very end of the article, Rémusat views the revolution as a necessary response to a society that had lost its way: a society in which there was no true respect for the throne or religion; a society in which both the elite and the people obeyed laws without caring about understanding them; a society dominated by habit, convention, frivolity, and passive obedience. Rémusat praises the revolutionary generation's striving for rational government while acknowledging its mistakes: "Their will was not commensurate with their understanding"; "because their opinions were favorable to the people, they assumed that the people thought as they did, and that their reason would suffice" (Rémusat, "De l'influence du dernier ouvrage" 34–35). Maintaining that the bad times were the revenge of those who were oppressed, he asserts the faith in the people that is fundamental to an understanding of *L'Habitation de Saint-Domingue:* "How painful it is to remember those sad times! How awful it is to think that the people who surround us—the people, whose fate occupies so many noble hearts and minds—hides beneath its apparent calm such a great capacity for crime! This idea would lead to desperation if reason did not remind us that the only way to preserve the multitude from its own furor is simply to make it happier, and that prudence and humanity both advise the same thing" (36). Those "sad times" explain Napoleon's rise to power for Rémusat. The people imagined that "Buonaparte, as odious as he turned out to be, was the person who was needed" (38). Gradually, the notion of equality that Napoleon used to manipulate the people was lost altogether, and an unending spirit of militarism took its place. It was only possible "for the work of the revolution to be accomplished" (44) and its principles to be preserved once there was an end to the reign of the man whom Staël called "the oppressor who lay like a pall over the human race" (Kadish and Massardier-Kenney 44).

Rémusat's position regarding Napoleon, who in 1802 rescinded the freedom that had been granted to slaves in 1794, strengthened his ties with the profoundly antislavery Staël family. Mme de Staël's father, Jacques Necker, and her mother, Suzanne Curchod Necker, had been members of the first antislavery organization, the Société des Amis des Noirs, in the 1790s. Moreover, Necker spoke out publicly against the abuses of slavery and addressed those abuses in his published works beginning in 1784, before Wilberforce's antislavery campaign in England; and, indeed, in his first speech to the British Parliament, Wilberforce invoked Necker's testimony (Berchtold 170–72). Staël's own efforts were later followed by those of her family members and immediate circle. Hugh Honour contends that there can be little doubt that she influenced, if she did not form, the abolitionist sentiments of her daughter, Albertine; her daughter's husband, Victor de Broglie; her son, Auguste de Staël; her onetime lover Benjamin Constant; and her admirer Sismondi (Honour 131). While Broglie vigorously defended the antislavery cause in the legislative arena, Albertine played a part by translating one of Wilberforce's short works on the slave trade in 1814 (Berchtold 173). Most important, however, were the efforts of Staël's son, who, up until the moment of his untimely death in 1827, conducted an extensive letter-writing campaign, traveled, published pamphlets, gave lectures, brought to the attention of the public instruments of torture used by slave traders, and even spoke directly to the king regarding the inhumane treatment of slaves.

In addition to his article about the French Revolution, Rémusat's own experiences and convictions drew him into the abolitionist circles in which Staël's family played such central roles. He spent a year from 1817 to 1818 in the Ministre de la Marine's Bureau de la direction des colonies. As he explains in *Mémoires de ma vie,* during that time he had access to all the plans, projects, memoirs, notes, alleged abuses, and judicial proceedings associated with the colonies. He wrote reports on notable events, including those that had occurred in Saint-Domingue. He gained further knowledge of those events in reading *Mémoires pour servir à l'histoire de la révolution de Saint-Domingue,* published in 1819 by Pamphile de Lacroix, who was part of the expedition whose defeat culminated in Haitian independence in 1804. His journalistic activities connected with antislavery were numerous. He wrote summaries of British newspaper articles, letters, and brochures about the slave trade and slavery for the *Journal de la Société de la morale chrétienne.* In September 1824, a long, unsigned article, which contains many elements evident in *L'Habitation de Saint-Domingue,* appeared in *Le Globe;* a series of antislavery articles signed C.R. appeared in that newspaper in 1825 and 1826 (Goblot xxii–xxiv).

Rémusat was also a leading participant, along with Broglie and Auguste de Staël, in the Committee for the Abolition of the Slave Trade, which had been formed by the Société de la morale chrétienne at the time of its creation in 1821. By maintaining a special library, the committee sought to influence public opinion regarding antislavery. The members of the Société de la morale chrétienne, which included the future Orléanist king Louis-Philippe, belonged to a political and social elite, many of whom were Protestants. Following the model of British benevolent societies, and relying heavily for information and assistance on British abolitionist individuals and organizations, that society sought to promote charitable acts of all sorts, including the better treatment of slaves and the abolition of the slave trade. Its goals were moral and social. Its causes were those of the oppressed: prisoners, the poor, slaves, the Greeks fighting for independence against the Ottoman Turks, and others. On their behalf, the society called for the kind of ameliorations that are discussed in Rémusat's play: antitorture measures, Sunday as a day of rest, access to the sacrament of marriage, religious education, appropriate health measures for pregnant women. Although it is true, as we shall see, that Rémusat strives in *L'Habitation de Saint-Domingue* to be impartial and eschew antislavery polemic, it is also true that his sentiments at the time of writing the play were in line with those of other antislavery activists of his time and that he sympathized with the condition of enslaved Africans. Writing to his mother in 1819, he states, "The violence that the blacks committed was more justifiable, that is less of an injustice, than the excesses of our Terror" (Riegert 128).

The literary significance of *L'Habitation de Saint-Domingue* is closely related to the social and political context in which it was produced. An essential part of that context was the rise of French Romanticism. With the shift in power toward the ultras, and with increased censorship of the press and other oppressive political measures, the gap that had divided young royalist and Catholic writers such as Victor Hugo, Alphonse de Lamartine, and Alfred de Vigny from liberals such as Rémusat, Charles-Augustin Sainte-Beuve, and Benjamin Constant narrowed. The coming together of the two groups—one revolving around the more conservative newspaper *La Muse française,* the other around the more liberal *Globe*—produced the unified revolt against classical prescriptions for poetry and tragedy that is known as the Romantic movement. What these writers shared was a rejection of the Bourbon policy of *union et oubli,* whereby national unity required forgetting the past, and in particular the revolutionary and republican past. As Alan B. Spitzer describes the generation that came of age in 1820, "The *esprit révolutionnaire* [the revolutionary spirit] was not to be confounded with the *esprit né de la révolution* [the spirit born from the revolution]—what the former had undertaken, the latter was to consolidate. The mission of the fathers was to destroy, that of the sons to conserve" (Spitzer 187). Doing so entailed the freedom to look back at their country's national past and to represent that past in the form of tragedy. It is not surprising, then, that the French Romantics rebelled against the rules of classical theater, which required the depiction of universal subjects such as those drawn from antiquity and the use of an elevated language far removed from modern historical realities. Although literary history typically singles out Hugo for having articulated the goals of Romantic theater in his *Préface de Cromwell,* published in 1827, and having transformed French theater with the performance of *Hernani* in 1830, the development of historical drama was common to his whole generation. Along with Rémusat's plays, such drama includes works by Vigny, Lamartine, Prosper Mérimée, Alexandre Dumas père, and others. These authors sought to produce serious drama that would compete with the growing appeal of melodrama among modern spectators.

Rémusat expressed views on theater on a number of occasions. As early as 1820 he published the essay "Révolution du théâtre" in the *Lycée français*. That essay was one of the first attempts to formulate a plan for theatrical reform, as Rémusat himself noted in republishing it later in *Passé et présent*. He was an active collaborator in the project that began in 1822 to publish *Chefs d'oeuvre des théâtres étrangers*. And in 1828 he published a review of Hugo's *Cromwell* in *Le Globe*. Calling for a thoroughgoing overhaul in theatrical principles and practice, Rémusat seeks a middle ground between the old and the new. Theater in verse is preferable, although not a requirement, he states repeatedly. In prose or poetry, in tragedy or comedy, however, dramatic language must be simple and natural. He calls for the depiction of events that affect real people and for a range of characters drawn impartially in all their complexity. In the place of classical abstraction or the exaggeration of good and evil, he seeks to treat modern history accurately and thus speak directly to a broad range of citizens in post-revolutionary society. Such ideas were new and influential, as Sainte-Beuve observes: "Many of the most visible and notable literary figures took heed and fell into line. How many distinguished people of the time who saw themselves as heads of the movement, and who are to an extent, had to be tugged along . . . in their literary judgments. Through his daring and innovative criticism, which was often conveyed through his conversation, M. de Rémusat consistently served as one of the 'tugboats' of the movement, although the public was frequently not aware of him" (Sainte-Beuve 941).

Fundamental to the view of historical drama that Rémusat and other members of his generation articulated was the achievement of Shakespeare. In an article written in 1830, Rémusat emphasizes the special relationship that Shakespeare holds with his audience, which derives in large measure from the fact that his theater is written in a natural language accessible to all classes of his contemporaries. In England, he observes, theater is native, popular, and local, not forced to obey the artificial tastes of an aristocratic elite; there, "a theatrical representation is a popular celebration" (Rémusat, *Passé et présent* 211). Instead of limiting speech to members of the nobility, who can only speak to their equals on stage, Shakespeare allows members of society to converse across class lines. The English know the affairs of their country; they are curious and knowledgeable about their past. As the literature of Walter Scott as well as Shakespeare shows, they revel in the charm of their ancient practices and beliefs. In contrast, the French people have been excluded from representations of their own past. The fault lies not with the playwrights, Rémusat states, but with the absolutist governments under which they wrote: "Our tragedy has thus been like our history, and our history like our government, and our government like our society" (214). He concludes that the political condition of a nation is intimately connected to its theater; and that freedom, patriotism, and national drama go hand in hand.

Although written in prose, *L'Habitation de Saint-Domingue* conforms in most respects to Rémusat's ideas for theatrical reform. Serious dramatic effect is produced through simple speech; and persons drawn from all social ranks, including the lowest, engage in meaningful dialogue. Indeed, Rémusat presents the full panoply of social classes that Denis Diderot called for in the eighteenth-century *drame bourgeois:* the planter and his family, the overseer, persons of color, house and field slaves, slaves born in Africa and those born in the colonies, or Creoles. The language is free of such neoclassical euphemisms, which Rémusat decries in his review of *Cromwell,* as the generic word *pastor* for a priest. Instead, Rémusat calls one of the major characters in *L'Habitation de Saint-Domingue* by the more culturally specific designation *curé.* Historical events do not serve merely as background but constitute the substance of the drama. Geographical specificity plays a crucial role: for example, because Rémusat's work is situated at Le Cap in the north of Haiti, where the colonists were confronted by rebellious blacks, as opposed to the south and west, where mulattoes had greater control, characters representing the class of persons of color have relatively little importance in the play (Goblot xxvi–xxvii). Conditions of plantation life such as the harvest of sugarcane and the preparation of sugar are not only mentioned but used in ways that affect the characters and the plot: for instance, the accident in which Old Roger is maimed fuels the fire of the slaves' willingness to rebel. Most important, perhaps, Rémusat rejects the classical concept of *bienséance*. Although Jean-Jacques Ampère praised the play in his letter to Mme Récamier, he did not fail to mention how shocked he was by its Shakespearean mixing of tones and genres: "Often we are revolted by the juxtaposition of comedy with scenes of total realism" (Ampère). Rémusat himself calls the play, with its depiction of the atrocities committed during the revolution and its allusions to subjects such as rape, "a bit raw" (Goblot xv). It is perhaps understandable, then, that, having first read the play in a salon in which no women were present, Rémusat did not seek to present it on the stage.

An analysis of the play itself requires a brief summary of its plot. *L'Habitation de Saint-Domingue* enacts a slave uprising modeled after the events that occurred in Saint-Domingue beginning on August 21, 1791. Life on the plantation of the Valombre family—Monsieur, Madame, son Léon, and daughter Célestine—is disrupted when a representative of the Assemblée nationale, M. de Tendale, arrives to examine the condition of the slaves and preach their eventual liberation. Imbued with eighteenth-century philosophical thought, Léon welcomes de Tendale's talk of freedom. However, he gradually realizes the discrepancy between philosophy and the reality of his family's economic interests. At the same time that de Tendale, the Valombre family members, and the local curé

are debating the treatment of slaves and the admissibility of their
eventual emancipation, rebellion is brewing on the plantation. The
leader, the runaway slave Timur, desires justice for his enslaved
fellow workers, but he also seeks revenge for personal reasons.
His beloved, the African slave Hélène, was raped by Léon, who
continues to pursue her. After a confrontation in which Timur attacks Léon, Timur is captured. Léon now faces his father's order
to punish Timur, his own guilt for having wronged Timur, and the
blacks' demand that Timur be freed. Violence breaks out. The
plantation is burned, M. and Mme de Valombre are killed, and the
other principal white figures—Léon, Célestine, and the Curé—are
captured. Now it is Timur who is placed in the middle of competing
forces: his need to punish Léon, the blacks' bloodthirsty desire to kill
the whites, resistance to his leadership by some blacks, and the re-
alization of the heavy demands that newly found freedom places on
him and the other insurgents. Against Timur's wishes, the blacks
kill the Curé. When Timur is about to wreak vengeance upon Léon
by raping Célestine, who has by now lost her mind, Hélène inter-
venes. Despite their mutual hatred, the two men swear to protect
each other in the face of the ferocious mob that seeks to destroy
both of them. But when the mob kills Célestine, Léon leaps to his
death into the ocean. Timur exhorts the other blacks to follow him
at the end of the play.   theory & Reality of freedom

The dramatic unity of this seemingly disparate plot can perhaps
best be defined in terms of a conflict between theory and reality—
more specifically, between abstract and concrete notions of freedom. Léon and Timur, whose evolutions as characters tie the play
together, ultimately resolve the conflict by facing up to the success
of the slave insurrection, although what that success means for the
future remains uncertain.

In Act I, Léon stands alone in advocating the French revolutionary discourse of freedom, without realizing the contradiction
between the rhetoric he is mouthing and the reality of the plantocratic society in which he lives. In contrast, his sister and the

Curé articulate the pragmatic reality of ameliorating the conditions of slave life. Ironically, although, as noted earlier, the word *curé* names a specific religious presence in the French colonies, in his abolitionist outlook and actions the Curé resembles British clergymen more than French priests.

In Act II, Timur solitarily encourages armed revolt by the blacks without realizing the extent to which his compatriots are as yet unable or unwilling to follow his lead.

Act III marks a turning point in several respects. There is a major change in Léon. He observes the contradiction between de Tendale's rhetoric, which he himself had espoused in the first act, and the economic reality of slavery as articulated by his father. He also grapples with the affective reality of his feelings for Hélène. Célestine now not only stands for a pragmatic understanding of the condition of slaves; she also represents the voice of reason when she describes the conflict that Léon confronts: "I'm afraid you're going to have to choose between your principles, on the one hand, and our plantation, on the other." The outbreak of violence also brings the reality of slavery to the fore and clarifies the position of several of the characters. The Curé and de Tendale, like Rémusat himself according to Sainte-Beuve (933), retain a firm faith in the instincts of the people, their errors and limitations notwithstanding. Seeds of doubt are sowed in Léon's mind concerning his values and past actions as he listens to Hélène express her hatred for him. Timur similarly learns that his revenge must be sought against Léon, not her.

In Act IV, Léon now represents the pole of reality, as opposed not only to de Tendale, but also to his ultra father, who persists in denying the impending danger of the slave revolt. A parallel evolution occurs with Timur, who increasingly understands the depth of irrationality and will to violence among his fellow slaves. At issue between the two chief protagonists, Léon and Timur, at the end of this act is which side will prevail: Léon's culpable white system, or Timur's black insurrection, which is itself not blameless.

In Act V, the actions of each of the chief protagonists and the ultimate resolution of the play are prompted by a woman. On Timur's side, it is Hélène who prevents him from moving to the dark side of slave irrationality and violence in his desire for revenge. On Léon's side, it is the murder of Célestine that impels him to end his life as the sole survivor of the plantation which has been destroyed. Hélène now embodies the voice of reason that Célestine had represented earlier in the play. In a similar reversal, Timur now is left to face the conflict between the theory and reality of revolution that Léon grappled with earlier. Although black agency wins out, the outcome is uncertain and problematic, as the course of history would prove the Haitian revolution to be.

It is worth noting that those present at the reading of the play report that originally it ended differently. In that version, de Tendale is captured and undergoes an evolution whereby he recognizes the reality of the slaves' aspirations. As he exhorts Timur to restore order among the rebels, white soldiers arrive and a peaceful solution is reached. In exchange for the release of Léon, his sister (named Albertine instead of Célestine in this version), and the Curé, de Tendale assures Timur that he will arrange for the emancipation of the blacks. Although it is difficult to explain the modifications in this original version, of which no written text exists, it seems probable that upon reflection Rémusat wanted to acknowledge black agency: that is, to acknowledge that it was the will of the blacks, not that of the French, that decided Haiti's outcome.

There are several groups of characters in *L'Habitation de Saint-Domingue* whose significance bears further consideration: the parents (M. and Mme de Valombre), the main feminine characters (Célestine and Hélène), and the masculine protagonists (Léon and Timur).

It is characteristic of Rémusat's dramatic approach that no simplistic judgment can be formed about what the Valombre parents represent in *L'Habitation de Saint-Domingue,* although in the balance it is clear that with respect to the issue of antislavery, they signify the problem, not the solution. On the positive side, Jean-René Derré observes that at one level they are just average, honest people: "the husband hardened by the practices of his milieu and reasoning like his peers while undoubtedly being more worthy than many of them; the wife, a good mother, whose very mediocrity makes her believable" (Derré xlv). Rémusat attempts to treat them objectively and to avoid reducing them to representatives of a greedy, unfeeling planter class. On the negative side, however, the father espouses the very ideas of the former colonists and Restoration ultras that elsewhere in his writings Rémusat blames for past and present political problems in France and the colonies. In his correspondence, Rémusat called colonists the "ultras of the tropics" (Goblot xxvii). Not surprisingly, the Valombres' name connotes the valley of shadows *(val d'ombre).* Their actions are driven by economic forces, and up to the moment of their death they lack lucidity about the present or the future. Willing to send their children to France to be educated, they care little about the Enlightenment lessons the children learned there and have no insights into what revolution means for their country or their family.

The two feminine protagonists, Célestine and Hélène, conform largely to the class, race, and gender stereotypes of the time, but only up to a point. At one level, Célestine is a typical young, naïve white girl, who has been protected from the harsh realities of plantation life. The play begins with her dismay at the escape of her bird, an act that foreshadows the flight of the runaway slaves, or maroons, who cause the insurrection. Her lack of understanding of the profound nature of the slaves' dissatisfaction, juxtaposed with her superficial, short-term attempts to alleviate their suffering, suggests how limited the effectiveness of her philanthropic gestures are. She dutifully obeys her mother, making such silly comments about a slave being whipped as: "In France one would never allow it! ... Well, I suppose if one must, one must... If not, mammá surely wouldn't let them." Although her sentimentalism is an appropriate response to slavery, Célestine fails to go to the root of the problem, which is her mother's disempowered role within the family and the economy. Both mother and daughter subscribe in principle to a gentler ethos of paternalism that emerged in the late eighteenth and nineteenth centuries. However, neither possesses the understanding or the power to bring about the necessary imposition of that ethos in the place of the older model of patriarchy, which requires "obedience, discipline, and severity" (Morgan 258–59).

Yet Célestine is far more than just a silly girl. She may be unable to effect change, but she is eager to expand her knowledge of the political context in which she is placed, asking her mother if she may read Rousseau and reminding her brother that she understands the concept of the rights of man. As noted earlier, she also serves in the first acts of the play as the voice of reason, a role that is dramatically reversed when she loses her reason in the closing acts. In the early version of the play that Rémusat later revised, Célestine was reportedly named Albertine. Significantly, Albertine was the name of Mme de Broglie, Germaine de Staël's daughter (Goblot xviii). Perhaps when Rémusat thought of the exercise of reason in a feminine mode, it was the example of the Staël family that came to mind. One must also remember that he was raised and educated by Claire de Rémusat, whose *Essai sur l'éducation des femmes* was published by Charles after her death, around the same time that he was writing *L'Habitation de Saint-Domingue.* In that work, Claire de Rémusat describes women as less methodical, philosophical, and steady in their judgments than men; but she attributes to them the same humanity, reason, will, faculties, morality, and freedom. Moreover, she claims that they have certain superiorities: observation, intuition, sense of detail, faithfulness, and a moral sense. She considers Rousseau a friend of women and approves of the post-revolutionary movement that he promoted toward restoring conjugal and filial sentiments. Although approving of the move to bring women back to the home, where they can raise their daughters and love their husbands, she disagrees with Rousseau regarding women's education. The formation of a free and moral woman, which is what Rémusat's Célestine has the potential to be, was the chief goal of his mother's view on the education of women. She also believed that educating daughters went hand in hand with educating mothers: as we can see in the play, both Célestine and Mme de Valombre would have profited from greater maternal enlightenment.

In the case of Hélène, one again meets a character who both resembles and differs from early-nineteenth-century feminine stereotypes. She is modeled after the depictions of the beautiful, victimized African woman Néali, whose story became a standard trope in abolitionist writings. First evoked by the Scottish explorer Mungo Park in his *Travels in the Interior Districts of Africa,* published in 1799, Néali was the focus of the winning submission in 1823 for a competition sponsored by the Académie française and won by Victor Chauvet. Apologizing to the "white daughters of Europe" for the indelicate details of slavery that he describes, Chauvet points the finger at the lecherous slave trader Belmar (Chauvet 3). That name, and the evil force it represents, resonates throughout nineteenth-century writings about blacks; "Delmar" in Hugo's *Bug-Jargal* is an example.

Rémusat, however, differs considerably with respect to women's issues from Chauvet or Hugo. As noted above, his intellectual formation occurred at the knees of two strong intellectual women, Germaine de Staël and his mother. It is not surprising, then, that Hélène is far more than a victim. In one crucial scene in Act III, she scorns Léon and finds the words not only to denounce his actions but to articulate her rejection of everything that his plantocratic privilege represents. By using her own and Timur's real non-slave names (Badia and Touko), she affirms her African culture; and she refuses to take advantage of the master's attraction to her, as some of the other slave women encourage her to do. At the end of the play, she is the one who brings Timur back to the path of moral rectitude. Not only does she prevent another rape, in this case of Célestine; she also brings a tone of moral superiority to bear on the revolutionary cause that the rebels will pursue as the play comes to an end. Hélène in the second half of the play, like Célestine in the first half, has recourse to the exercise of reason to provide the male protagonist with a moral compass as new and confusing circumstances surround him.

A similar complexity marks the treatment of the male protagonists, Léon and Timur. Léon is depicted as naïve, in contrast with his father, who understands the economic realities of the slave system that Léon never really questions or rejects. And, in contrast with de Tendale and the Curé, who both see blacks as capable of enlightenment and improvement, Léon can be called a racist inasmuch as he, unlike his Enlightenment predecessors, denies the slaves' natural rights (Rétat liv). At times his hypocrisy and racism are rendered in a comic mode, as when he mistreats his domestic slave Jean-Jacques while bragging to de Tendale that he named his slave for Rousseau. At other times, his conduct is depicted in the mode of tragedy, as in the monologue in Act II that reveals the extent to which lust dominates his sentiments and degrades his character. Even his change of heart, beginning with Act IV, when he realizes that the rape has sullied the honor of Timur, has more to do with his own white, *ancien régime,* patriarchal value system than it does with the injustice he has committed or the rights of black people. In the last act, he perhaps responds to the Curé's admonition to "delve deep within ourselves" for divine pardon. Perhaps he dies with remorse for his actions, although the impulse to die with his sister and preserve the honor of the massacred family seems to predominate.

Despite his failings, Léon is not the evil villain who in sentimental literature is pitted against the virtuous hero. A young man torn between the forces of freedom as theory and as practice, he is somewhat akin to Rémusat and others of his confusing postrevolutionary generation. Moreover, like Célestine, Léon is a dutiful child. If patriarchal authority has condoned abuses, as it most often did on plantations, the fault lies with the patriarch, not with the son who feels duty-bound to obey him. Even his racism is complex: although in theory he denies the natural rights of blacks, in practice he has feelings for a black woman—a fact that de Tendale, showing himself to be more racist than Léon, finds unthinkable. Rémusat's choice to end the play with Léon leaping into the ocean holding his sister is significant. Notwithstanding his evolution during the course of the play, Léon's character is ultimately too negative for this act to confer heroic stature upon him. Rather, he dies as the representative of a doomed family and social system that he was too young to fully understand or to change. His death preserves that family's honor, but it does nothing to modify the *ancien régime* values that led to their annihilation.

Just as Léon is denied heroic stature in the play, so too is Timur. His lack of lucidity in the first acts of the play matches Léon's: he is willing to blame Hélène for her rape, an act which, as he surely would have known, was part of the routine abuse of black women by white men. And he is willing to seek revenge by subjecting Célestine to the same crime, without reflecting upon the injustice and violence that such a retaliatory act would represent. Also, like Léon, he has difficulty reconciling theory and practice. Although he wants to end the domination to which whites have subjected the slaves, he respects the Curé, who wanted to see him married to Hélène; and up to the end, it is clear that, as his fellow slaves claim, he has one foot in the value system of the white masters. As a further qualification of his heroic persona, he gradually must learn about the realpolitik of revolution. The choices he makes when he gains control of the black rebels are problematic, as he himself understands: in Jean-Paul Sartre's words, revolutionary change requires "dirty hands." Torn between the need to be responsive to the slaves, whose cause he represents, and the need to forge ahead militarily and economically, in ways that they hardly understand, he remains a solitary and tragic figure at the end of the play.

There is little doubt that Timur stands as an avatar of the revolutionary leader Toussaint Louverture: Sainte-Beuve referred to the play as "Rémusat's Toussaint Louverture" (Sainte-Beuve 945–46), and in his *Mémoires,* the author himself compares it to Lamartine's play of that name (Goblot xx). The date of the slave uprising depicted in *L'Habitation de Saint-Domingue* is the date when the slave Toussaint Bréda, who later assumed the name of Louverture, appeared on the scene. Until June 1802, when Napoleon had him arrested and imprisoned in France, Toussaint grappled with the very issues that Rémusat depicts Timur struggling with in the play. In the years preceding his death in 1803, after political and military successes had been achieved, Toussaint was increasingly resented by blacks who saw his demands for high levels of agricultural productivity as close to a form of reenslavement. The kind of opposition that Timur has to confront is modeled after events in Toussaint's struggle to lead the liberated rebels: in 1801, he ordered the execution of his adopted nephew, Moïse, who gave voice to the slaves' demands. Moreover, Toussaint's desire to see the return of white émigrés, who possessed agricultural knowledge that he valued, made blacks question where his allegiances lay, as is similarly the case in Rémusat's play. One of the reasons why Timur frees Léon is that he needs Léon's help. Unlike his less practical co-conspirators, he realizes that the future of Saint-Domingue will involve a series of struggles in which whites will inevitably play a role.

To conclude, what is perhaps most important to keep in mind in reading *L'Habitation de Saint-Domingue* is the author's liberal politics and the play's composition in 1825. As noted earlier, the ultras tried to block the recognition of Haiti, which liberals saw as a crucial step toward eventual abolition of slavery in the French colonies. Despite the opinion of moderates and most former colonists themselves, ultras persisted in denying the reality of slavery, just as their counterparts had done in 1791. Liberals such as Rémusat placed the blame for the past violence that blacks were driven to commit squarely on the shoulders of self-deceived colonists who refused to ameliorate intolerable conditions on plantations. This is Rémusat's perspective in the play. His idea is "to bring about reforms, not revolutions" (Goblot xxxii). Although readers may not think of such an idea as abolitionist in the modern sense of the word, it is important to remember that immediate emancipation began to be advocated in England, France, and the United States only in the 1830s and 1840s, at least a decade after Rémusat's play was written. For its time, it is a forward-thinking, enlightened text that puts crucial political events in an interesting and innovative historical and literary form.

WORKS CITED

Ampère, Jean-Jacques. "Lettre à Mme Récamier." 1825. *Correspondance et souvenirs*. 2nd ed. Paris: Hetzel, 1875. 352–54.

Arlet, Jacques. *Charles de Rémusat: Mémorialiste, grand témoin du XIXe Siècle*. Paris: Remi Perrin, 2003.

Berchtold, Alfred. "Sismondi et le groupe de Coppet face à l'esclavage et au colonialisme." *Sismondi Européen*. Ed. Sven Stelling-Michaud. Geneva: Slatkine, 1973. 169–221.

Chauvet, Victor. *L'Abolition de la traite des noirs*. Paris: Firmin Didot, 1823.

Derré, Jean-René. "Rémusat et le théâtre en 1825." In *L'Habitation de Saint-Domingue; ou, L'Insurrection*. By Charles de Rémusat. Ed. J. R. Derré. Lyon: CNRS, 1977. xxxv–xlvii.

Goblot, Jean-Jacques. "Genèse et signification de 'L'Habitation de Saint-Domingue': Charles de Rémusat et la révolution." In *L'Habitation de Saint-Domingue; ou, L'Insurrection*. By Charles de Rémusat. Ed. J. R. Derré. Lyon: CNRS, 1977. xi–xxxiii.

Honour, Hugh. *The Image of the Black in Western Art*. New York: Morrow, 1976.

Kadish, Doris Y. "Hybrids in Balzac's *La Fille aux yeux d'or*." *Nineteenth-Century French Studies* 16.3/4 (1988): 270–78.

Kadish, Doris Y., and Françoise Massardier-Kenney, eds. *Translating Slavery: Gender and Race in French Women's Writing, 1783–1823*. Kent, Ohio: Kent State University Press, 1994.

Morgan, Philip D. *Slave Counterpoint: Black Culture in the Eighteenth-Century Chesapeake and Lowcountry*. Chapel Hill: University of North Carolina Press, 1998.

Ozouf, Mona. *Les Mots des femmes: Essai sur la singularité française.* Paris: Gallimard, 2001.

Rémusat, Charles de. "De l'influence du dernier ouvrage de Madame de Staël sur la jeune opinion publique." *Archives philosophiques, politiques, et littéraires* 5 (1818): 27–47.

———. *Passé et présent.* Paris: Didier, 1857.

Rétat, Laudyce. "Idéologies et colonisation: De Marmontel à Rémusat." *L'Habitation de Saint-Domingue; ou, L'Insurrection.* By Charles de Rémusat. Ed. J. R. Derré. Lyon: CNRS, 1977. li–lx.

Riegert, Guy. "'L'Habitation de Saint-Domingue; ou, L'Insurrection' de Charles de Rémusat: Un Langage truqué." *Esclavage et abolitions: Mémoires et systèmes de représentation.* Ed. Marie-Christine Rochmann. Paris: Karthala, 2000. 127–35.

Roldán, Darío. *Charles de Rémusat: Certitudes et impasses du libéralisme doctrinaire.* Paris: L'Harmattan, 1999.

Sainte-Beuve, Charles-Augustin. *Portraits littéraires.* Paris: Garnier, 1843.

Spitzer, Alan B. *The French Generation of 1820.* Princeton, N.J.: Princeton UP, 1987.

CAST OF CHARACTERS

MONSIEUR BOISTIER DE VALOMBRE,
  a colonist-planter, owner of La Goyave
  plantation in Saint-Domingue

MONSIEUR DE TENDALE, an envoy
  sent to Saint-Domingue by the
  Assemblée nationale

MADAME DE VALOMBRE

LÉON, Monsieur and Madame
  de Valombre's son

CÉLESTINE, their daughter

THE CURÉ

CÉSAR JULIEN, a mulatto

MORIN, a white, the plantation steward

MARIE-LOUISE, Célestine's
  longtime nursemaid

JEAN-JACQUES, Léon's servant

ROSINE, Madame de Valombre's
  servant   } *Household blacks*

HÉBÉ, another of her servants

GALAOR, a free black, in charge
  of the slaves

TIMUR, a carpenter ⎱
JEAN-PIERRE
JUAN
ALMANZOR
TÉLÉMAQUE   ⎬ *Field blacks*
VÉNUS
HÉLÈNE
HERMIONE
CLOTILDE   ⎰

Male and female blacks of various ages

The action takes place August 21–23, 1791, not far from
Cap-Haïtien, in Saint-Domingue, on La Goyave plantation.

The

SAINT-DOMINGUE
PLANTATION

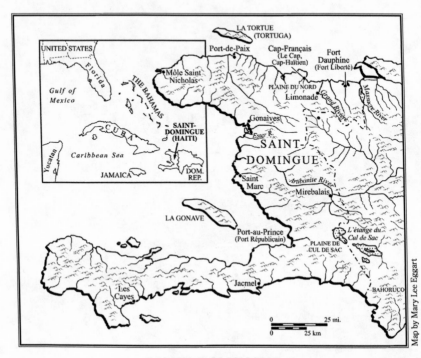

Map by Mary Lee Eggart

SAINT-DOMINGUE

ACT I

A raised, awning-covered veranda looking out over a sunny sugar-cane field. The left and right sides are protected from the sun by high trellises entwined with greenery and flowers. Upstage, a balcony, and above it a practical blind the width of the veranda. Down left, an open entrance. Against the trellis, left center, a wicker bird cage with several birds. Center stage, a dining table and four chairs. Close to it, down left, a chaise longue facing the footlights at an angle. Up left, a small table with a bell on it, and two chairs. Down right, another small table and two chairs. Tropical plants and flowers here and there.

At rise, Célestine is standing left, at the bird cage, distraught.

CÉLESTINE. Oh, good heavens, Marie-Louise! Where is she?

MARIE-LOUISE. Mademoiselle?

CÉLESTINE. My favorite... The parakeet with the fiery red feathers! She's gone! How can it be?

MARIE-LOUISE. Perhaps there's a hole in the cage, mademoiselle.

CÉLESTINE. Oh! And so tame, so sweet... And she loves me so! How could she...

MARIE-LOUISE. How indeed, mistress dear! Birds are born to fly, I'm afraid.

CÉLESTINE. But wasn't she happy? Each day I gave her a new branch to perch on! With flowers, Marie-Louise!

MARIE-LOUISE. She must have preferred the trees to perch on! Back in the forest. With her mother, mademoiselle. At home... Like those three blacks I saw this morning.

CÉLESTINE. Those what?

MARIE-LOUISE. Yes... The three they found hanging, at dawn, in the settlement.

CÉLESTINE. Goodness me! How frightful! Who ever did such a thing?

MARIE-LOUISE. Don't waste your pity, mademoiselle. They did it to themselves. They just wanted to go home, I imagine. Back to Guinea...

CÉLESTINE. To Guinea? What ever do you mean?

MARIE-LOUISE. Just what I say. When a wretched black dies, far, far away from home... If he has been good, his soul goes back to Guinea. Back to the coast... Everyone knows that!

CÉLESTINE. Come now, Marie-Louise. Surely you don't believe such things. After all I taught you when we were in France. You, a good Christian! You promised to get rid of such silly superstitions.

MARIE-LOUISE. I know. No more witch doctors, mademoiselle. But hanging is different. It's not as if they were poisoned. You see? And they did it to themselves. So there's nothing wrong...

CÉLESTINE. Really, nurse dear! It's always wrong not to do God's will. The good Lord brought them here, and this is where they were supposed to stay.

MARIE-LOUISE. Well, the good Lord will pardon them, I'm sure. They were so unhappy... When someone wasn't born here, don't you know... Even my mother... She was only a child when she came here, but she never stopped thinking of home, mademoiselle. And when she was just about to die, didn't she say to me: "You see that smoke? It's my father's hut..." She could actually see it.

CÉLESTINE. And you, Marie-Louise? Are you unhappy here too?

MARIE-LOUISE. Me? Oh no! This is my home. Besides, you are so kind, mademoiselle... So good to me... Nothing in the world would make me want to leave.

CÉLESTINE, *with a sigh.* Why aren't they all like you? They can be so difficult sometimes. *(At the bird cage.)* Bring me some water, would you? The birds are thirsty...

MARIE-LOUISE, *about to comply, stopping.* Oh, mademoiselle... Before we forget... It's almost time the sick ones were coming by from the infirmary. *(Pointing upstage.)* They'll be passing by any minute.

CÉLESTINE. Do you have the lemons and the laurel leaves I promised them?

MARIE-LOUISE. Yes, but it wasn't easy. I had to say they were for you, mademoiselle.

CÉLESTINE. Good. *(Listening.)* Oh, I think I hear them. Be a dear and raise the blind.

MARIE-LOUISE, *raising the blind, upstage, revealing the balcony, and peering out.* Yes... Here they come...

One can hear the confused murmur of a group of people.

CÉLESTINE, *going upstage, looking over the railing, greeting several members of the unseen group.* Good day, my friends... Ah! I see old Toby has recovered. *(With nods here and there.)* Monsieur... My friend... But what's this? Little Alphonsine is still limping?...

(Pointing.) And that woman... *(To* MARIE-LOUISE.*)* The one who had the baby... Oh, how weak... *(To the woman.)* You... How weak you are!... *(To* MARIE-LOUISE.*)* Please... Throw her some bread... *(After a moment.)* What is she saying?

MARIE-LOUISE. She says that they've put her back to work.

CÉLESTINE. What? So soon? That can't be! Does papá know? I'll speak to him... *(To the unseen woman.)* You poor thing!... If the steward were here I would tell him myself...

MARIE-LOUISE, *at the balcony.* Monsieur Morin, mademoiselle? *(Pointing over the railing.)* There he is...

CÉLESTINE, *returning downstage.* Well, we'll see about that!

MORIN'S VOICE, *from below.* Come on, you lazy good-for-nothings!

CÉLESTINE. I'll have a word with him.

MORIN'S VOICE. Get a move on! There's work to be done.

> *One hears the cracking of a whip and cries from the group.*

MARIE-LOUISE. Oh!

CÉLESTINE. My God! Is he whipping them?

MARIE-LOUISE, *calling down.* Run!... Run!

MORIN'S VOICE. You hear me?

> *The whip cracks again with more cries from the group.*

CÉLESTINE. How can he? *(Going to the railing, calling down.)* Monsieur! Monsieur Morin...

MORIN'S VOICE. Mademoiselle?

CÉLESTINE. May I have a word with you, monsieur? *(Returning.)* I'll simply never understand such things. Papá can scold me all he likes. In France one would never allow it!... *(With a little resigned sigh.)* Well, I suppose if one must, one must... If not, mammá surely wouldn't let them.

MARIE-LOUISE. That's right, mademoiselle. There's nothing like a little crack of the whip to get the work done!

CÉLESTINE. Oh? And what do you know, Marie-Louise?

MARIE-LOUISE. When I was your age, before I was your nursemaid, mademoiselle... I worked in the fields too, just like them.

MORIN *enters, down left, whip in hand.*

MORIN, *to* CÉLESTINE. Mademoiselle wishes to see me?

CÉLESTINE, *still upstage.* I do, monsieur! It's about that poor woman who had the baby. The one who just passed by...

MORIN, *approaching.* Ah! That big mulatto...[1] Did she say something to offend mademoiselle?

CÉLESTINE. No...

MORIN. Did she do something wrong?... She's usually a good worker. A little lazy now and then, but... I'll give her a talking-to if she—

CÉLESTINE, *interrupting.* No, no! It's not that, monsieur. On the contrary!

---

1. Mulattoes were persons of mixed French and African descent, who were usually free. In 1789, the slave population on Saint-Domingue totaled approximately 500,000, almost half of the 1 million slaves in the Caribbean. The number of free persons of color is estimated at 28,000, of whom more than half were mulattoes.

MORIN. Then...

CÉLESTINE. Good heavens! Her baby is ten days old, and they've just put her back to work!

MORIN, *misunderstanding.* Yes... Yesterday... She could have started sooner, but what's one extra day?

CÉLESTINE. But... I mean... Couldn't they let her rest another week? She's so sickly, monsieur.

MORIN. Rest? At a time like this? With the harvest and the pressing[2] going on day and night? We need all the hands we've got! Mademoiselle knows... *(About to launch into a tirade.)* Why, this very morning—

CÉLESTINE, *interrupting.* But how much work can a poor sick woman do? Please, monsieur...

MORIN, *with feigned consent.* How can I refuse mademoiselle? Even if she really is much too kind-hearted! She worries about these black folk more than they do themselves! Believe me, they're perfectly contented. That woman would never even think of complaining.

CÉLESTINE, *sadly.* No, I don't suppose...

MORIN. I knew mademoiselle would understand. Still, I promise to let her rest at night, despite all our work.

MADAME DE VALOMBRE *enters, down left.*

MADAME DE VALOMBRE, *to* CÉLESTINE. Good day, love... Give me a kiss. Are you feeling better since this morning?

CÉLESTINE, *trying to reply.* I—

---

2. "Pressing" is processing sugarcane in a press to extract the juice.

MADAME DE VALOMBRE. My, my... How pale you are! Are you sure you're not ill?

CÉLESTINE. Not at all. I—

MADAME DE VALOMBRE. Perhaps it was the wind... Is that it? The wind... It didn't let you sleep last night, and you're all tired out.

CÉLESTINE. But—

MADAME DE VALOMBRE. And having tea so late...

CÉLESTINE. Really, mammá.

MADAME DE VALOMBRE. Shall I give you something for it? A glass of water, love, with a little sugar?

CÉLESTINE. But I'm perfectly fine, I assure you.

MORIN, *to* MADAME DE VALOMBRE. Mademoiselle looks the picture of health, madame.

MADAME DE VALOMBRE. Are you sure, Monsieur Morin?... *(Moving to the chaise longue, changing the subject.)* But... Just now, you two were chatting. I'm sure she was asking for something. A favor for some black or other... She has such a kind heart, dear child...

MORIN. I was explaining to mademoiselle that her kindness can go too far... That, if we treated our blacks like our family, madame, as she would like, the plantation would soon go to rack and ruin... That a household needs order...

MADAME DE VALOMBRE. Of course... But that's how we Valombre ladies are, monsieur. Too kind, too kind... *(To* CÉLESTINE.*)* You see, love? One has to accept things as they are.

MORIN. Heaven knows that ours is anything but a cruel plantation. Why, I would rather leave if I had to treat our blacks like Monsieur

Gernon du Mont-Noir. Besides, Monsieur de Valombre would never permit it. *(Nodding to her.)* Nor madame...

MADAME DE VALOMBRE, *to* CÉLESTINE. Of course not, love. Our blacks are treated superbly. Monsieur Morin hardly punishes them at all. And he's right...

CÉLESTINE. But, just now...

MADAME DE VALOMBRE. It's not their fault if they're black, poor things...

CÉLESTINE. No, but...

MADAME DE VALOMBRE. It's your aunt in Paris. She must have filled your head with all kinds of lies about the colonies, *chérie.*

CÉLESTINE. Please, mammá, I wouldn't dream of criticizing. I was only asking a favor of monsieur, for a poor woman who just had a baby.

MADAME DE VALOMBRE. Oh? Well, in that case... *(To* MORIN.*)* You should do what she asks, monsieur. You can be a trifle harsh with our blacks! And that will never do!

MORIN. But madame... I protest...

VALOMBRE *enters, down left.*

VALOMBRE. Good day, everyone! *(To* MADAME DE VALOMBRE.*)* My sweet! *(To* CÉLESTINE.*)* Titine! *(To* MORIN.*)* And you! So, this is where you are! I've been looking for you all day, high and low! Even up in the coffee country...

MORIN. But monsieur, I never left the presses. At a busy time like this...

VALOMBRE. True... True... I'm not scolding, mind you. It's just that I would have liked to have a little stroll to discuss our affairs.

MORIN. Of course, monsieur.

VALOMBRE. The harvest is doing well, I trust?

MORIN. Splendidly! Why, we started only yesterday, but the cane is heavy as can be. Just as I expected. (VALOMBRE *gives several satisfied little nods.*) I can't say exactly, but I wouldn't be surprised if monsieur got a good two hundred eighty barrels of sugar...

VALOMBRE. Ah!

MORIN. Even three hundred... And, as for the syrup...

VALOMBRE. Three hundred barrels! I say! That should make our dealer at Cap-Français[3] happy! The one who's always complaining... (*To* MADAME DE VALOMBRE.) You hear, Sophie? Three hundred barrels!

MORIN. But monsieur, we're in desperate need of more hands. That fever that struck the blacks last month has severely reduced their numbers. And I have to inform monsieur that this very morning—

VALOMBRE, *interrupting.* I know, I know... Three of them hanged themselves...

MORIN. Yes... Fortunately only one of them was a good worker. Still, it cuts into the profit.

VALOMBRE. I should say! It's as if each one of those wretches robbed a hundred *louis* from my purse!

MORIN. Quite so, monsieur... Did monsieur also hear about the cow that was sick?

VALOMBRE. Hear? Hear what?

3. Situated in the north, the city that was named Cap-Français (Le Cap) during the colonial period is today Cap-Haïtien.

MORIN. That she died last night... Poor thing! It broke my heart to look at her... All swollen... A pathetic sight... Tsk tsk tsk! Pathetic...

VALOMBRE. Yes... Well, we'll get another one. But you're right about the blacks. We do need some new ones. Next week you'll go into town... *(Reaching into his pocket.)* In fact... *(To himself.)* Where did I put it?... Ah! *(Taking out a letter.)* Listen... *(Reading.)* "Cap-Français, etc. etc.... Monsieur, I have the honor of inform- ing you that, by the grace of God and fair winds, I have put in here on the sixteenth instant with a cargo of two hundred twenty pieces of the finest stock, pure black, two-thirds male and one-third female, to be placed on the block Monday the twenty-third at nine in the morning at the Hôtel de l'Ancre. If you wish to honor me with the confidence of a reply, etc. etc.... Jérémie Descroque, Cargomaster of the vessel *Human Kind- ness...*" *(To* MORIN.*)* Here, you take care of it.

MORIN. And does monsieur still have no news of our runaways?

VALOMBRE. I hope my son will have some for us. *(To* MADAME DE VALOMBRE.*)* I must say, Sophie, Léon is taking his time. He was supposed to leave Cap-Français early and arrive here in time for tea. What's keeping him, I wonder?

MADAME DE VALOMBRE. Please... I'm dreadfully concerned. I hope nothing is wrong.

> MORIN *fumbles in his pocket.*

CÉLESTINE. What could be wrong, mammá?

MADAME DE VALOMBRE. Heavens, love! An accident can happen in the wink of an eye. And your brother is so careless. The horse could bolt and—

VALOMBRE. Come now, my sweet! You and your imagination! I'm not worried in the slightest. But I do wish he would hurry. He knows I'm waiting for him with dozens of things to do. And tea time, after all...

MORIN, *to* VALOMBRE, *holding out an announcement.* Here, monsieur... The description of our two scoundrels... Would monsieur like me to have it posted?

VALOMBRE, *taking it, reading.* "Lindor, a Creole, between twenty and twenty-two years old, four feet eleven inches, somewhat stooped... No tattoos... A scar over his upper lip, three fingers missing from his right hand..."

MORIN. Quite exact, monsieur...

VALOMBRE, *continuing.* And the other... "A Wolof, between twenty-eight and thirty years old, five feet eight inches... The name Rex tattooed on his left shoulder... A cutlass scar on his right side... Rolls of flesh on both wrists and welts from lashes to the back, some quite fresh... Escaped during the night of the fifteenth to the sixteenth...[4] With any information please inform Monsieur Morin, steward of La Goyave plantation, Limonade parish..."[5] (*Approvingly, to* MORIN.) Perfect! I could pick them out of a thousand!

MORIN, *taking the announcement.* Monsieur has no other orders? I'd best catch up with my blacks. They've been alone too long...

4. The reference throughout the play is to runaway slaves, otherwise known as maroons (from the Spanish word *cimarrón*). They lived in forest communities throughout the Caribbean as well as in Central, South, and North America.

5. Limonade is a city in the north, 15 kilometers southeast of Le Cap. It was one of the centers of slave unrest.

VALOMBRE, *waving him off.* Please... *(As* MORIN *is about to leave, stopping him.)* Just one thing... If you see that any of them have the fever, be sure to send them to the infirmary. And quickly, you hear?

MORIN, *nodding.* Monsieur.

VALOMBRE. Damnation! I don't want to lose thirteen more of them, like last month! I can't afford it!

MORIN, *nodding, to* MADAME DE VALOMBRE *and* CÉLESTINE. Madame... Mademoiselle...

>   *He exits.*

VALOMBRE. There! No more business today, my dears... I'm all yours. Just the two of you. *(Sighing.)* Ah... They can say what they like. There's nothing but home and family to comfort good folk like us.

>   *He crosses right and sits down at the table.*

CÉLESTINE, *approaching him.* Papá dearest...

MADAME DE VALOMBRE, *to* VALOMBRE. Give the child a kiss, *mon cher.* Aren't you proud to have such a beautiful daughter?

CÉLESTINE. Oh, mammá!

>   VALOMBRE *complies.*

MADAME DE VALOMBRE. Now I'm going to rest a bit. *(She moves to the chaise longue, then stops.)* Heavens! Just listen to that wind! Célestine, love... *(Pointing upstage.)* Be a dear and lower the blind.

CÉLESTINE. Yes, mammá... *(Upstage, about to do so, looking out over the railing.)* Oh, look! It's my brother...

She waves into the distance as MADAME DE VALOMBRE *comes and joins her.*

VALOMBRE. Léon?

He stands up and joins them.

CÉLESTINE. Goodness, how he's galloping!

MADAME DE VALOMBRE. The poor child must be mad!

CÉLESTINE. Here at last...

MADAME DE VALOMBRE. I'll give him a good talking-to, that one! *(Ringing the bell on the little table, up left, calling.)* Rosine... Rosine...

VALOMBRE, *impatiently.* Well? What's taking him so long? Can't he get off his horse?

CÉLESTINE. He's coming up the stairs, papá.

As she lowers the blind, ROSINE, *a black, enters.*

ROSINE. Madame?

MADAME DE VALOMBRE. Go fetch some water and sprinkle the blinds. And fetch me my fan.

ROSINE. Very good, madame.

She curtsies and exits.

VALOMBRE. Well? *(As* LEON *enters.)* Ha! It's about time, young man! Your mother has been worried about you.

LEON. Sorry, papá... *(Nodding.)* Mammá...

MADAME DE VALOMBRE *gives him a kiss as* CÉLESTINE
withdraws demurely upstage.

MADAME DE VALOMBRE. Good heavens, child! You're burning up!
Go change your clothes...

LÉON. No need, really... It's just the sun and the dust...

VALOMBRE. What on earth kept you? We've been waiting for hours.
At least, I hope you have some news for me.

LÉON. Oh yes, papá! And important news too. That's what kept me.
I couldn't leave...

VALOMBRE. Oh? Tell me...

LÉON. Let me catch my breath.

MADAME DE VALOMBRE, *to* VALOMBRE. Please, *mon cher...* Let him...
(*To* LÉON.) Take your time, son... Sit down...

As *he takes a seat at the little table, up left, she reclines on
the chaise longue.* ROSINE *enters, gives her a fan, and goes about
sprinkling the blinds, left and right, during the following dialogue, listening as* MADAME DE VALOMBRE *fans herself.*

VALOMBRE. Well? Has anything come from France?

LÉON. Yes... A ship...

VALOMBRE. And the *Gazette*?[6] Did you read it?

LÉON. I should say I did!

VALOMBRE, *impatiently.* And? And?

---

6. The *Gazette du jour,* founded in November 1790, became the *Moniteur colonial.* It had ceased to exist by August 1791.

LÉON. The revolution, papá!... It's raging on all sides... The people are growing stronger and more victorious day by day! Ah, to be in France at a time like this!

VALOMBRE, *unenthusiastically.* Oh? Perhaps... Details, son... Tell me everything!

LÉON. I have only a general idea, papá. But you can read it all in the *Gazette.*

VALOMBRE. Indeed...

LÉON. What might interest you most, though, and what especially delights me, is the fact that a representative sent by the Assemblée nationale[7] has landed.

VALOMBRE. Landed? Here?

LÉON. At Cap-Français... I saw him... I spoke to him...

VALOMBRE. Sent by the Assemblée—

LÉON. Ah, what a gentleman, papá! Compared to his kind, we're mere children... Mere amateurs... Why, when I listen to the likes of them, it's as if... *(Growing excited.)* as if I were sitting transfixed...

VALOMBRE. And why is he here, this representative of yours?

LÉON. Why, papá? What a question!... To spread the revolution, that's why. Why else? I've told you a hundred times...

VALOMBRE, *with a hint of good-natured sarcasm.* Yes... *(Aside.)* At least...

7. The Assemblée nationale is the lower house of the French parliament. In 1789, that body, known as the Assemblée nationale constituante, put an end to royal absolutism and laid the groundwork for the French Revolution. No commissioners were actually sent to Saint-Domingue by the Assemblée nationale until November 22, after the slave uprisings.

LÉON, *continuing, more and more agitated.* But you've never wanted to believe me...

MADAME DE VALOMBRE. Please, child...

LÉON, *impassioned.* You don't want to believe that despotism is gasping its last... In both worlds, papá... That we can't preserve a despotic regime in ours when the motherland herself has thrown hers off!

> ROSINE *curtsies and exits.*

VALOMBRE. Léon...

LÉON. That it's absurd for us to maintain a baseless system and obey the minions of the Court! *(He stands up.)* It's time for us to stand tall, to hold our heads high... Time to have our own governing body, our own elected assembly...

VALOMBRE, *trying to calm him.* Come, come, Léon...

LÉON. Time to have all the rights of free men, papá!

VALOMBRE. And you got all that from your representative?

LÉON. All that and more! But you'll see for yourself. And you'll hear him. He's coming to visit.

VALOMBRE. Coming? Here?... Who told you?

LÉON. He did. When I saw him at the Cercle du Commerce... Yesterday... He said how much he wanted to see the colonial system up close... To visit a large plantation, papá... So I stood up, and I told him then and there that ours... my father's... was one of the largest and finest to be seen...

VALOMBRE. Indeed!

LÉON. ...and that we would consider it an honor if he would come spend a day... That he wouldn't find the luxurious life of the towns, but only a family of good, honest citizens with simple habits and the joys that family and philosophy can bring...

VALOMBRE. Quite! *(Aside.)* Philosophy...

LÉON. He shook my hand and said: "Fine, my young friend. I accept." And he's coming tomorrow.

VALOMBRE. Damnation! Our blacks will be working at the presses tomorrow... He'll miss all the beauty, all the majesty of seeing them laboring in the fields. We'll have to arrange it. I'll tell Morin.

LÉON. No need, papá...

VALOMBRE. Oh?

> MADAME DE VALOMBRE *lets her handkerchief fall to the floor and rings the bell she is still holding.*

LÉON. I passed him coming in and mentioned it to him.

VALOMBRE. Ah... I see...

> HÉBÉ, *a black woman, enters.*

MADAME DE VALOMBRE, *pointing to her handkerchief.* My handkerchief, Hébé...

HÉBÉ. Yes, madame.

> *She picks it up and gives it to her.*

VALOMBRE, *to* LÉON. I'm sure you wouldn't give up this little visit for an empire's worth of gold, young hothead!

MADAME DE VALOMBRE, *to* HÉBÉ, *waving her off.* You can go now.

HÉBÉ. Very good, madame.

She curtsies and exits.

LÉON, *replying to* VALOMBRE. Of course not! Just think. We're on the verge of a... a rebirth! *Our* rebirth, papá! Our liberty is dawning... We, the people... Until now I played no role. I could only join with the liberators of France in my mind, in my spirit! But now I can enjoy the fruits of their example. I can follow their lead... Ah! This is the most beautiful day of my life!

VALOMBRE. Careful, Léon! Revolutions are frightful things. When they begin no one knows where they might end! This representative of yours seems quite reasonable for the moment. He wants to observe conditions for himself. He wants to talk with me... Nothing could make more sense. But will he be able to rein in the movement once it has begun?

LÉON. Ah, papá! Can one ever go too far on the road of reason and liberty?

VALOMBRE. Look at France, my son. Hasn't much already happened that those who set things in motion never dreamed of for an instant? Yes, many abuses have been undone. But how? And at what cost?

LÉON, *interrupting.* Papá...

VALOMBRE, *continuing.* How much violence, how much injustice has been committed by those benefactors of humanity of yours!

LÉON. Bah! Isn't the cause all that matters? Doesn't it make up for every excess?? For everything? Think of the ten centuries of "violence" and "injustice" that have to be atoned for! It's just as the poem says... Two lines I read the other day...

"After ignoble woes, justice it is,
When suffering slave casts off those bonds of his!"

We're slaves, papá, and we must be free!

VALOMBRE. Yes, well... Speaking of slaves, Léon, do you have any news of my two runaways?

LÉON. Alas, no. Not a word. I looked in at the prison myself, but they weren't there either. In fact, there's a good deal of concern. The number of runaways has been increasing lately, but the authorities are determined to stop treading lightly. They've decided to hunt them down, bring them to justice, and not give an inch.

VALOMBRE. Indeed!

LÉON. They regret now that they spared those three other runaways... The ones that they captured, armed to the teeth!

CÉLESTINE, *who has been following the conversation, up left, timidly.* Then you think those three slaves were wrong, brother dear?

LÉON. Wrong? I should say! Scoundrels, brigands, uncontrollable rebels... Wretches who would corrupt an entire population if they had the chance!... No punishment can be too severe to put down revolt. It's a crime, Célestine. High treason against society...

CÉLESTINE. But... I thought... *(Quoting.)* "Justice it is when suffering slave casts off those bonds of his!"

LÉON. There's no comparison! Wretches like those? And our property besides... *(Stopping short, changing his tone.)* No, no... You can't fool me, sister dear. Here I was, about to give you a serious answer when you're having your little joke!

CÉLESTINE, *timidly, almost inaudibly.* But...

LÉON, *to* VALOMBRE, *continuing.* Yes, papá... Despite my sister's questionable attempts at humor, I'm sure you'll catch those two good-for-nothings. And when you do, I advise you to show no mercy. To one of them especially... Timur, the carpenter...[8] An insolent barbarian if ever there was one!

VALOMBRE. Well, I hope that all your talk about the revolution didn't keep you from taking care of my affairs in the town.

LÉON. Certainly not, papá. I have principles, after all. To serve one's country best one first must be sure to have order in his household. That's why I say, unless we keep order these blacks will be our masters when all is said and done. Thank heaven, from now on things are going as they should. No more abuse of power, no more favored treatment... A just system of laws, with freedom and equality for one and all... And one that will make our rebellious slaves quake in their boots!

CÉLESTINE, *timidly.* But...

LÉON. Speaking of that... Our gentleman from Paris has told me that they're going to begin by proclaiming the rights of man![9]

MADAME DE VALOMBRE. Please, Léon... You must be starving. You and your father can talk politics over tea.

LÉON. Of course, mammá. Whatever you say... *(Approaching* CÉLESTINE *and taking her hand, as* MADAME DE VALOMBRE *rings the bell.)* And you, sister dear...

CÉLESTINE, *coyly.* How good of you to notice me. Is it also one of the rights of man not even to ask his sister how she is?

---

8. Some slave men were singled out for education as trained artisans.

9. On August 26, 1789, the Assemblée nationale issued "La Déclaration des droits de l'Homme et du citoyen" ("The Declaration of the Rights of Man and of the Citizen").

LÉON. Excuse me, Titine. My head was so full of so many things!...
Please... Tell me, has anything interesting happened while I
was away?

CÉLESTINE. Oh yes! Something frightful!

LÉON. Oh?

CÉLESTINE. My favorite parakeet... The one with the fiery red feathers... She's escaped... Flown off...

LÉON. And you're angry?

CÉLESTINE. Of course! How could she? She loved me so!

LÉON. Ah! *(Teasing.)* Like the runaway black... "Justice it is when
suffering slave..."

CÉLESTINE. Oh! How can you... My parakeet? A slave?

LÉON, *laughing.* Just tit for tat, sister dear... Tit for tat...

ROSINE *enters.*

MADAME DE VALOMBRE. Rosine, serve the tea.

ROSINE. Very good, madame. *(As she curtsies and turns to leave.)* And
what shall I tell the *bon père,* madame?

MADAME DE VALOMBRE. The Curé?

ROSINE. Yes, madame. He's downstairs. He wants to come in.

MADAME DE VALOMBRE. Good heavens! *(To* VALOMBRE.*)* We'll have
to invite him to stay for tea.

VALOMBRE. Of course... *(To* ROSINE.*)* Show him up.

ROSINE. Very good, monsieur.

She exits.

LÉON. Oh, that bore! Who needs him?

CÉLESTINE. But he's so kind... And he means so well.

LÉON. Him and his ideas! Always groaning about the misery of the blacks... The cruelty of the rich... So tasteless, so unreasonable...

CÉLESTINE. Oh?

LÉON. So tedious...

VALOMBRE. True, our churchly friend has no head for business...

LÉON. Not the slightest...

VALOMBRE. He spent years on the mainland, among all those Spaniards.[10] And he's brought their ideas with him, though they're utterly out of place. Simply not for us...

> ROSINE *and* HÉBÉ *enter and begin setting the table, center.*

LÉON. Life on the plantation is already too free. And now, with all these priests who want to baptize the blacks and let them go to church on Sundays... Next thing you know they'll want to get them married!

VALOMBRE. Indeed...

LÉON. With all their talk about "loving thy neighbor" they won't rest until they've run all the landowners into the ground!

> THE CURÉ *enters with two black domestics, who remain at the door.*

---

10. It is not clear whether Rémusat refers here to Europe or to Louisiana, which was controlled by the Spanish. The Spanish were generally less severe than the French in their treatment of slaves.

THE CURÉ, *to* VALOMBRE. Good day, my friend. Please excuse this rather untoward visit.

VALOMBRE. What a pleasure...

THE CURÉ. I hope I am not intruding.

VALOMBRE. Of course... Of course...

THE CURÉ. And I trust you are well?

VALOMBRE. Quite well, *mon père.*

THE CURÉ. Delighted, monsieur... And Madame de Valombre?... And mademoiselle?

MADAME DE VALOMBRE, *as* CÉLESTINE *curtsies.* Quite well, thank you...

THE CURÉ. Heaven be praised, my friends. And Monsieur Léon? (*To* LÉON.) I saw you on the road a little while ago, monsieur. Riding like the wind. I am afraid you did not see me.

LÉON. Perhaps. I always try to look straight ahead.

CÉLESTINE, *offering* THE CURÉ *a chair from upstage.* Won't you sit down, *mon père?*

THE CURÉ. Thank you, mademoiselle. You are too kind. *(Sitting down.)* By the way, I was happy to do your little errand of mercy.

CÉLESTINE. My little...?

THE CURÉ. The blind old mulatress...

CÉLESTINE. Ah...

THE CURÉ. I am sure she will remember you in her prayers, mademoiselle.

MADAME DE VALOMBRE, *getting up and motioning the others to the table, center.* Come...

> *She and* VALOMBRE *sit down, followed by* LÉON *and* CÉLESTINE.

VALOMBRE. Won't you join us for tea, *mon père?*

> MADAME DE VALOMBRE *waves* ROSINE *and* HÉBÉ *off. They curtsy and leave.*

THE CURÉ. You are too kind, monsieur. It would be an honor... But that really is not why I am here. I would not have disturbed your tea were it not for a rather pressing matter.

VALOMBRE. Oh? Please... Tell me...

THE CURÉ. If I may, monsieur. You will pardon me, I trust... (*Nodding to* MADAME DE VALOMBRE.) And you, madame... *(Continuing.)* I know you are going to say that I always sing the same tune...

LÉON, *under his breath.* Ha!

THE CURÉ, *continuing.* ...but I have no choice. It is my sacred duty to spread a message of peace and kindness... A message of divine charity, monsieur... Even at the risk of annoying my listeners.

VALOMBRE, *objecting weakly.* Not at all, *mon père.*

LÉON, *under his breath.* Not at all!

VALOMBRE. I assure you...

THE CURÉ. And so I hope you will not think it too bold of me... It is with the greatest respect, believe me... But it is stronger than I am, and I would hardly be able to say my prayers in good conscience this evening if I did not—

VALOMBRE. Yes... Please...

LÉON, *to* THE CURÉ, *impatiently.* You were saying, *mon père?*

THE CURÉ, *replying.* You are very young, Monsieur Léon. But when you are my age... Or if you were in my place today, you would understand that I am only doing as my duty demands. *(To the others.)* That is why, my worthy parishioners... (LÉON *represses a little yawn.*) That is why I pray you let me intercede in favor of two poor slaves whom I met not far from here...

LÉON, *under his breath.* No doubt...

CÉLESTINE, *to* THE CURÉ. What about them, *mon père?*

THE CURÉ, *continuing.* One, an old man, and the other a young woman. They were bound to one another at the wrists, and were about to receive thirty lashes...

LÉON. Thirty?

THE CURÉ. The old man, that is...

LÉON. Impossible!

THE CURÉ, *continuing.* ...because I do not recall how many for the negress.

CÉLESTINE. How frightful!

THE CURÉ. My memory worsens by the day, I am afraid.

LÉON, *to* THE CURÉ. Impossible, I tell you! The law says no more than twenty-nine.[11] And we observe it to the letter.

VALOMBRE, *to* THE CURÉ. And what would you have me do, *mon père?* A plantation without discipline...

11. In 1685, Louis XIV issued the Code Noir, which regulated the practices of slavery in the French colonies. Although some may have believed otherwise, it placed no limit on the number of lashes that could be inflicted.

CÉLESTINE. Poor things! (*To* THE CURÉ.) What did they do?

THE CURÉ. I asked them. (*To* VALOMBRE.) It seems the old man talked back to your steward, monsieur. And the young woman refused to work.

VALOMBRE. Why, that's insubordination!

CÉLESTINE. But thirty lashes, papá!

LÉON. Twenty-nine... Twenty-nine...

VALOMBRE, *to* CÉLESTINE. Please, Titine...

LÉON. And not one more!

THE CURÉ, *to* VALOMBRE, *replying.* Yes, monsieur. I understand. And I am not asking that they not be punished for it. Truly, they have erred... And I would be the first to preach obedience to their master. Does Saint Paul not tell us that all power comes from God, my friend, and that patience and resignation are Christian virtues? But I appeal to your good heart, monsieur. To your spirit of charity... Take pity on them... Madame... Mademoiselle... They are God's creatures, just as we are!

LÉON. Creatures? Yes... Creatures, indeed!... Mindless creatures, without intelligence, without reason... Unable to understand the simplest abstract thought!

THE CURÉ. I could not agree less, Monsieur Léon. Whenever I have been permitted to explain the Gospel to the blacks, their minds have understood, for their hearts have believed...[12] Besides, even the most simple are belovèd of Our Lord.

---

12. Among the many arguments for the intelligence of blacks, the abolitionist abbé Henri Grégoire published *De la littérature des nègres* in 1808. His enlightened views on the treatment of blacks may have inspired Rémusat in the creation of the character of the Curé.

LÉON. Oh yes! Yes! *(Standing up.)* That Gospel of yours crams their heads full of lovely ideas!

CÉLESTINE, *standing up.* Brother dear...

LÉON, *continuing.* They learn that there are other duties than obeying their masters' wishes! They learn to have a conscience... And all that, just so that you can spread your power at the expense of ours!

VALOMBRE, *standing up.* Léon! That's enough!

THE CURÉ. No! Let the young man speak. I can see how much the poor child has strayed... How much the philosophy of our time has warped his judgment's innate perfection. *Scientia inflat,* Saint Paul tells us. "Knowledge puffeth up!" And that so-called philosophy of his is so overblown with pride that it can hardly be concerned with the pains of the oppressed. Whereas we—

LÉON, *interrupting, sharply.* Rubbish!

VALOMBRE. Léon!

LÉON. To hear him speak, you would think it's *our* philosophy that oppresses! The philosophy that delivers mankind from the rule of the despots... And from the tyranny of the priests!...

CÉLESTINE. Please, brother dear...

LÉON, *pacing nervously.* The very ones who, everywhere they go, degrade their fellow men, and who come here to sow the spirit of rebellion, say what they will!

THE CURÉ. Nothing of the kind, my young friend. You are mistaken, if I may be so bold... We do not preach the spirit of rebellion. God forbid that we should ever counsel the lowly in any but the ways of humility. But humility is the duty of the great as well. And it requires that they allow the poor idolaters in their charge to share the message of the Gospel. *(Standing up.)* For you can be sure. The masters will answer for the salvation of their slaves...

LÉON, *archly.* I say, monsieur! If you think you can frighten us... This is the eighteenth century, my friend! You can't lull us to sleep with your pious nonsense!

VALOMBRE. Really, Léon!

LÉON. We who live in the age of Voltaire and Rousseau don't tremble to hear your—[13]

CÉLESTINE, *interrupting.* I beg you, brother dear! Don't say such wicked things!

THE CURÉ, *to* CÉLESTINE. Thank you, dear child. Your support is precious. It is quite clear that monsieur has suckled at the century's bosom. I pray you explain my point of view to your esteemed parents.

CÉLESTINE. Oh yes, *mon père,* with all my heart! *(To* VALOMBRE *and* MADAME DE VALOMBRE, *in turn.)* Please, papá!... Please, mammá!... Spare those poor souls... *(Growing more and more impassioned.)* For me, if you love me... For... For the love of God!

MADAME DE VALOMBRE. Célestine...

CÉLESTINE, *continuing.* If you knew how much it hurts me when I think that there are creatures... Suffering creatures, parents dear... Human beings... And that I could save them from their pain if only...

---

13. The famous Voltaire and Jean-Jacques Rousseau were French thinkers of the Enlightenment. Voltaire advocated religious and social tolerance and was known as a crusader against prejudice and tyranny. Rousseau's philosophical and political concepts were central to French revolutionary thought. Leaders including Maximilien Robespierre were especially drawn to Rousseau's notion of a republic of virtue.

MADAME DE VALOMBRE, *standing up and whispering to* VALOMBRE. Really, *chéri...* We mustn't let the child carry on so. Frail as she is...

THE CURÉ, *to* CÉLESTINE. May heaven reward you, mademoiselle!

MADAME DE VALOMBRE, *continuing.* It could make her ill...

VALOMBRE, *replying in a whisper.* We'll see... We'll see. *(To* CÉLESTINE, *aloud.)* Good heavens, child! I'm not a brute... If we didn't have to... Believe me, I would—

LÉON. Nor am I, sister dear! Everyone knows I loathe tyranny and the rule of despots...

CÉLESTINE, *to* VALOMBRE, *mistaking his remark for consent.* Ah! Thank you, papá!

LÉON, *continuing.* But weakness is an abomination!

CÉLESTINE, *not listening to* LÉON, *continuing.* I knew my father was a kind and gentle soul.

> *One hears the sharp crack of a whip outside followed by a piercing cry, continuing throughout the following exchanges.*

MADAME DE VALOMBRE, *looking around.* What...?

CÉLESTINE, *suddenly realizing what is happening.* Oh no! It's not... But I thought...

THE CURÉ. Already?

CÉLESTINE. God help them!

LÉON, *going upstage, raising the blind and looking out, to* THE CURÉ. Goodness me, *mon père...* It's that old protégé of yours... They're teaching him a lesson. *(Sarcastically.)* Next time you would do well to come plead for him sooner!

THE CURÉ, *to* VALOMBRE, *emotionally.* Please, monsieur... I thought you said...

> *As the cracking of the whip and the cries continue,* CÉLESTINE, *in a semi-swoon, staggers and falls onto the chaise longue.*

MADAME DE VALOMBRE. Good heavens! Célestine! (*To* VALOMBRE.) Help her!... *(To* LÉON, *as* VALOMBRE *rushes to the chaise longue.)* Help her!

> THE CURÉ *stands crossing himself and praying silently.*

LÉON, *rushing to her side.* Titine!

CÉLESTINE, *rebuffing them both.* No, no... I'm fine, mammá... It's nothing... Only those cries... Those frightful screams...

MADAME DE VALOMBRE. Of course... And so sudden, so shocking... Look... *(She holds out her quivering hands.)* I'm trembling too, love.

CÉLESTINE. Mammá...

MADAME DE VALOMBRE, *to* VALOMBRE. Please, *chéri*... Tell them to make him stop. Those screams will drive me out of my mind...

LÉON, *to* CÉLESTINE. Sister dear...

> *The cries grow more intense.*

CÉLESTINE. It's horrible... Horrible... (*To* VALOMBRE.) You promised, papá... You said...

VALOMBRE. But don't you understand, child? Once they've begun, to stop would be an attack on Morin's authority.

CÉLESTINE, *to* LÉON. Please, I'm begging you... Do something...

LÉON. He's right. Order must be preserved. Nothing is more important...

CÉLESTINE. It's too cruel, too cruel!... *(As* MADAME DE VALOMBRE *embraces her.)* Oh, mammá...

MADAME DE VALOMBRE. There, there, love... I know... I was that way too at your age. But try to understand... Try to be an adult...

VALOMBRE, *to* MADAME DE VALOMBRE. You see? We should never have let her go live with my sister...

MADAME DE VALOMBRE, *to* CÉLESTINE. There, there...

VALOMBRE. She's too Parisian for her own good now!

MADAME DE VALOMBRE. Don't scold, *chéri...* *(To* CÉLESTINE, *as the cries stop abruptly.)* Listen! They've stopped. Now no more tears, love...

LÉON, *to* CÉLESTINE. You see? We're not so heartless!

CÉLESTINE, *to* THE CURÉ. *Mon père... Mon père...*

THE CURÉ, *to* LÉON. I shall hold my tongue. This sweet child's tears say much more than I ever could. *(To* VALOMBRE.) And you, monsieur. Will you let this atrocity continue?

VALOMBRE. We'll see... *(He rings the bell.)* We'll see... *(Aside to* LÉON, *pointing to* CÉLESTINE.) Please, son, try to calm her.

A male black enters.

LÉON. Titine...

VALOMBRE, *to the black, softly.* Go tell Monsieur Morin to move away from the house...

The black nods and exits. After a few moments, THE CURÉ, *upstage, looks out over the balcony.*

THE CURÉ, *to* VALOMBRE. I do not know what you told him, monsieur... But they are tying the poor woman down!

CÉLESTINE. What?

THE CURÉ. God help us! They are ripping her clothes!

CÉLESTINE, *to* LÉON. What did he say?

THE CURÉ. Oh, shame and disgrace! Bloodthirsty beasts!

He covers his eyes and turns aside.

CÉLESTINE. Papá!

VALOMBRE, *to* LÉON, *pointing.* Lower the blind!

LÉON, *to* THE CURÉ, *crossing upstage.* You couldn't just be still? You had to tell us? *(Looking out, to himself.)* Ha! There she is, the rebel... *(Peering in sudden disbelief.)* What?... No, it can't be!... Not her... It's... It's Hélène!... *(Shouting.)* Stop! Good God in heaven!... Stop! Stop!... Not her!

All of a sudden he jumps over the railing.

VALOMBRE. Léon!

MADAME DE VALOMBRE,   *together:*   Son!

CÉLESTINE,   Brother dear!

VALOMBRE *and* MADAME DE VALOMBRE *rush to the railing.*

VALOMBRE. What the devil...

LÉON'S VOICE. Stop, I tell you!... Not that one!

MADAME DE VALOMBRE, *looking over the railing.* Thank God he's
not hurt!

LÉON'S VOICE. Not her! Not her!

THE CURÉ. So he does have a heart after all! *(Crossing himself.)*
Praise heaven!

End of Act I

ACT II

A space in front of the plantation house, unseen beyond the footlights. In the background, distant mountains, and up left, a low hill. Stage right, the entrance to the shed where the cane is pressed. Down right, a path leading offstage. Stage left, several low slave huts, set at an angle. Down left, a path leading to the house. Up left, a path leading off. Up center, at the foot of the hill, a tall stake in the ground. Tropical trees here and there.

At rise, male and female blacks are bustling about. An old black man has just been freed from the stake and is being carried off by his companions. Hélène, a young black woman, is still bound to the stake. Morin and Galaor, the black slave-guard, are looking on.

MORIN, *to the groaning black, as he is taken away, up left.* That should teach you a lesson, insolent wretch! (*To* HÉLÈNE.) And you, my lazy beauty!... Thinks she's the mistress, does she! (*Mimicking.*) "I won't work! I won't work!"

HÉLÈNE, *proudly.* And I didn't!

MORIN. Well, we'll see!

HÉLÈNE. You couldn't make me...

MORIN. You'll pay for it!

HÉLÈNE, *continuing.* And you won't... *(Sneering at him.)* You won't!

MORIN. No faces, thank you! *(He rips off her kerchief.)* Now, show us your pretty shoulders! *(Tearing off her tattered blouse and flinging it to the ground, exposing her bosom. To* GALAOR, *who is holding a whip.)* Are you tired, Galaor?

GALAOR. Not at all...

MORIN. Good. Then begin...

> As GALAOR *readies the whip,* LÉON *appears, down left.*

LÉON, *shouting.* Morin!

MORIN. Ah, monsieur! Come watch this lovely young—

LÉON, *running over, interrupting, to* GALAOR. Don't you dare! *(To* MORIN.*)* You hear me? *(Brandishing his riding crop, to* GALAOR.*)* If you so much as touch her...

MORIN. But...

LÉON. Thank God I'm not too late!

> *He frees* HÉLÈNE *from the stake.*

MORIN. But monsieur...

LÉON, *to* HÉLÈNE, *picking up the blouse and kerchief and handing them to her.* Cover yourself, my dear.

MORIN. What are you... *(Correcting himself.)* What is monsieur doing? Did his father give him permission? Monsieur knows I'm the only one who—

LÉON, *sharply.* Quiet! I do as I please!

MORIN. Begging monsieur's pardon, but... I and I alone have the authority...

LÉON. Quiet, I said!

MORIN. But... This young woman is guilty of insubordination, monsieur. And she must be punished.

LÉON. Guilty? This child? And a punishment like this?... It's unspeakable, my friend! You dare to treat these creatures so? These human beings? Like you and me? *his humanity shows*

MORIN, *shocked.* Holy mother of God! What are you... What is monsieur saying? Please... *(Softly.)* Not in front of the blacks!... We'll stop... *(To* GALAOR.*)* Put down the whip, Galaor. *(To* LÉON.*)* There... Only, for God's sake, monsieur should mind his tongue when they're listening.

LÉON, *calming down.* Yes... Perhaps I went too far. But I'm sure you understand.

MORIN, *to* HÉLÈNE. There, there, my child. We only wanted to frighten you. *(Raising his cane to the others, who have been watching and listening with interest.)* Enough! Back to work, all of you!

> *Cringing, they return to their various labors. Some go in and out of the pressing-shack with sheaves of cane or buckets of molasses. Down right,* VÉNUS, CLOTILDE, *and* HERMIONE[1]— *the last with an infant in a sling around her neck—are seated on the ground, weaving baskets.*

1. Slaves were stripped of their African identities and given Europeanized names, which were often drawn from classical literature or mythology. Rémusat calls attention to this naming practice by providing the African names of the characters Timur and Hélène: Touko and Badia.

VÉNUS, *as* HÉLÈNE *approaches, right.* You can thank your lucky stars, Hélène! If not for the young master...

> MORIN *stands about overseeing the work as* LÉON *remains center, by the stake, musing.*

TÉLÉMAQUE *down right, by the women.* Saved? By that one?... There's always a first time!

HERMIONE. It's not hard to guess why, Télémaque!

MORIN, *to* LÉON, *approaching, center.* Pardon me, monsieur...

HÉLÈNE, *to* HERMIONE, *reacting to her remark.* Oh? And what does that mean, may I ask?

MORIN, *to* LÉON, *continuing.* I'm glad monsieur agrees that he may have gone too far...

HERMIONE, *to* HÉLÈNE, *replying.* Come now, Hélène!

MORIN, *to* LÉON, *continuing.* I hope he'll excuse me. *(Slyly.)* I had no idea...

VÉNUS, *to* HÉLÈNE. It's plain as day, child!

MORIN, *to* LÉON, *continuing.* I mean, one can't always guess such things!

TÉLÉMAQUE *to* HÉLÈNE. Plain as day!

MORIN, *to* LÉON, *continuing.* Heaven knows, if he had told me I would never have dreamt of offending her...

LÉON. Please... Let it pass...

MORIN. I assure monsieur that, in the future... *(Pointing to* HÉLÈNE, *down right.)* I shall treat her more gently!

HERMIONE, *to* HÉLÈNE. If Timur were still here he wouldn't be too happy!

MORIN, *to* HÉLÈNE, *approaching.* Since you tire so easily, my dear, I'll have you weave baskets. *(Pointing.)* With them...

HÉLÈNE, *scarcely listening to him, to* HERMIONE. Ah! Timur...

She sits down with the others.

MORIN, *continuing.* And if you're a good girl, and if you behave, I'll give you a pretty cotton skirt next Sunday.

HERMIONE, *to* HÉLÈNE. You can be sure. Timur would rather see you whipped to death, he would...

MORIN, *to* LÉON, *joining him, center, holding out his hand.* So, Monsieur Léon... No offense, I trust...

LÉON. None...

MORIN. Only... Monsieur should be more careful, if I may say. All these folk have seen us, and—

LÉON, *archly.* I can take care of myself, monsieur!

MORIN, *under his breath.* Insolent pup!

He and GALAOR *exit into the shed, right.* TÉLÉMAQUE *follows them at a distance.* LÉON *begins pacing about, casting frequent glances at* HÉLÈNE.

LÉON, *to himself.* Damn! Such a pretty thing... Can it be that I...

HERMIONE, *to* VÉNUS. You see how he looks at her?

LÉON, *to himself.* Is it possible? Me...

VÉNUS, *to* HERMIONE. And how she pretends not to notice!

LÉON, *to* HÉLÈNE, *approaching her, embarrassed.* You know, Hélène...
What you did was wrong, and you deserved to be punished.
You know that, don't you? *(She looks away.)* Look at me when
I'm speaking! *(He bends down to make her turn her head, but no
sooner does he touch her than he pushes her away as if disgusted
with himself.)* No! What's got into me!

> THE CURÉ *enters, down left.*

THE CURÉ. Ah! Monsieur Léon... There you are! *(Pointing up, over
the footlights, in the direction of the veranda of Act I.)* They are
all waiting for you.

LÉON. Yes... I... I'm coming... And they're angry with me, I suppose...

THE CURÉ. Angry? Why? Because you jumped down from the balcony?

LÉON. I... I thought...

THE CURÉ. You did give Madame de Valombre a bit of a fright. But
a young man as agile as you... No harm, thank God! Besides, it
was a noble and spontaneous act, and one that does you credit,
my friend.

LÉON, *sadly ironic.* You think so, do you?

THE CURÉ. If you could see your sister, monsieur! The poor child
is weeping tears of joy.

LÉON. Oh?

THE CURÉ. And, as for me, I can only ask you to forgive the rather
unpleasant observations that I allowed myself to voice. After
all, preaching comes naturally to the likes of us. But I knew...
I was sure that you had a good heart! Come, they are all impa-
tient to see you.

LÉON. Yes, well...

THE CURÉ. Come...

LÉON, *following him off, down left, with a glance at* HÉLÈNE, *shaking his head.* Such a pretty thing!

They exit as the women, down right, continue their weaving.

HERMIONE, *to* VÉNUS. Yes! Plain as day! (*To* HÉLÈNE.) No need to keep denying it... We all saw him.

HÉLÈNE, *sharply.* No, no! I told you...

VÉNUS. Then why are you so angry? Where's the harm?

HÉLÈNE. I'm not!

VÉNUS. Good for you! (*Pointing to* HERMIONE.) She's only jealous, that one!

HERMIONE. Me? I beg your pardon! I'd never let a white man... And my master to boot!

CLOTILDE. Especially him! A cruel one like that!

VÉNUS, *to* HERMIONE *and* CLOTILDE, *sarcastically.* Ha! Not easy to please, you two! At your age I knew better. I was sold three times before I was eighteen, and I slept with all of them!

CLOTILDE. I'm sure! (*Good-naturedly.*) You old whore, you! You're a Creole, you are.[2] Not a good African, like us.

HERMIONE, *pointing to* HÉLÈNE. And she's from the coast. You would think she would know better. But she's gone and forgotten her Timur already. The one she calls Touko...

2. Derived from the Spanish word *criollo*, *Creole* is used here to refer to persons of African or European heritage born in the New World.

HÉLÈNE. Forgotten him? My Touko?

HERMIONE. Good God! It's obvious...

VÉNUS. Plain as day!

HERMIONE. I'd be ashamed to death if I were you.

CLOTILDE, *to* HERMIONE. You mean, you have no one to forget?

VÉNUS. Oh, but she does! She does!... And they all want her to forget them!

HÉLÈNE *stands up, dropping her basket to the ground.*

HÉLÈNE, *to herself, sighing.* Ah, Touko!... Poor Touko! Where are you, I wonder?

CLOTILDE, *to* VÉNUS. Why on earth is she so sad? If I were the one, it would never bother me!

VÉNUS. Maybe because it's not really true. Maybe she only wishes—

HERMIONE. Don't be silly! I'm telling you. I saw them together... Her and the young master... Hiding in a clump of banana trees...

CLOTILDE. No!

HERMIONE. Yes! The same night that Timur escaped...

HÉLÈNE, *overhearing.* What? My God...

VÉNUS. You hear that, Hélène? You hear what she said?

HÉLÈNE. But... No! It's not true...

HERMIONE. It's not true that monsieur took you into the banana trees one night?

HÉLÈNE. But...

CLOTILDE. "But... But..." Of course it's true!

HERMIONE. And not to catch hummingbirds, I'm sure!

VÉNUS, *to* HÉLÈNE. Did you have a good time, *ma petite*?

CLOTILDE. Did she?... Damn! I'll say...

HÉLÈNE. No, no... It's not true!

CLOTILDE, HERMIONE, *and* VÉNUS *laugh.*

CLOTILDE. Of course not!

HÉLÈNE. Oh! *(Aside.)* I can't bear it!

HERMIONE. See how embarrassed she is!

Her infant begins to squeal and cry in the sling around her neck.

CLOTILDE, *pointing.* The child, Hermione... While you sit chattering he's screaming to be fed.

VÉNUS, *as the squeals increase.* He wants mammá's nipple...

HERMIONE, *calming the infant.* I know, love... I know...

VÉNUS, *as* HERMIONE, *none too discreetly, begins nursing.* He's Galaor's, isn't he?

HERMIONE, *very matter-of-fact.* No... Jean-Pierre's...

VÉNUS. Jean-Pierre's? You told me Galaor's...

HERMIONE. Jean-Pierre's! I should know!

VÉNUS. You should! But how can you be so sure?

CLOTILDE, *to* HERMIONE. You told me Galaor's, too.

HERMIONE. I must have lost track.

HÉLÈNE, *still standing off to the side, lost in thought, to herself.* Will he ever come back?

CLOTILDE, *to* HERMIONE. Well... Whoever's...

HÉLÈNE, *continuing.* If only I knew where he was... I would run away and find him!

> MORIN *and* GALAOR *enter from the shed, followed by* TÉLÉMAQUE *and several male blacks.*

MORIN, *to* GALAOR. It's almost sunset and time to stop, Galaor... Except for the ones who are working through the night.

GALAOR. Poor devils! The ones on the presses are asleep on their feet.

MORIN. Lazy good-for-nothings! Only forty-eight hours... What right have they to be tired? On the smaller plantations they make them work three or four nights in a row. And without a wink of sleep! *(To the blacks sitting and standing about.)* You're soft, all of you! Not a backbone in the lot of you! *(To* GALAOR.*)* And it's our fault, my friend. *(To the blacks.)* We treat you too well!

GALAOR. Believe me, old Roger could barely stand up in there...

MORIN. So? What do you care? You're not doing his job!

GALAOR. No, but I am doing mine! And if I don't stay awake, who's going to crack the whip?

TÉLÉMAQUE *to* GALAOR. You? All you do is watch us work and puff on your cigar.

MORIN, *menacingly.* And if those are my orders, swine...

TÉLÉMAQUE, *retreating.* Oh...

MORIN. If he does what I tell him... Is that any business of yours?

TÉLÉMAQUE. No, no, master... None...

He hides behind the others.

MORIN, *to the women, right.* Now then... Your baskets... (*Examining them, to* VÉNUS.) Yours is going well, Vénus... (*To* HERMIONE.) But you... Still lazy as the day is long... Always with a baby hanging from your teat! Babies, babies! Forever making babies... We should see to it that you can never make any more! Who needs them? The trade is glutted with blacks these days... Just be sure you finish your basket by morning, even if you have to stay up all night!

HERMIONE, *under her breath.* Bah!

MORIN, *to* HÉLÈNE, *changing his tone.* And you, my dear... You haven't had time yet. I know... But next time... Next time... (*Chucking her under the chin.*) No need to be concerned... (*To the men standing about.*) And the rest of you? Why are you just standing about doing nothing? Out of the way! (*Pacing up and down.*) Out of the way, I tell you! (*Pointing to several jugs lying on the ground.*) And who left those? What are they doing there? (*Brandishing his cane.*) Get rid of them, you hear? Get rid of them! (*As the men hurry to comply, an anguished cry is heard coming from the shed.*) What in the name... (*Pointing.*) Télémaque, go see.

> *As the cries continue,* TÉLÉMAQUE *turns to exit into the shed but is prevented from doing so by* JEAN-PIERRE, JUAN, *and several other blacks entering from it.*

JEAN-PIERRE, *pointing right.* There's one in there who won't be working tonight!

MORIN. What?... Who, Jean-Pierre?

JEAN-PIERRE. Old Roger. He fell asleep and got his hand caught in the press. He's bobbing around in the molasses vat, monsieur.

MORIN. Clumsy damn fool! Are the rest of you bloody idiots going to do the same? Here's something that's sure to keep you awake! *(He flails the air here and there with his cane as the blacks grumble indistinctly.)* Do I hear any objections?

TÉLÉMAQUE. None, master... None...

JUAN. We were only thinking...

MORIN. Go on... You were thinking...

JUAN, *continuing.* ...that maybe the ones who work all night shouldn't have to work all day too.

> *The others voice their agreement with appropriate exclamations like "Yes, yes!" "That's right!" etc.*

MORIN. Silence! The first one to speak will be put in irons!

JUAN. But... Poor old Roger, master...

GALAOR, *to* MORIN. Maybe he was a little too old for the job.

MORIN. Then he should have known how to do it better!

JEAN-PIERRE. But at his age...

> *The others grumble their agreement.*

MORIN. Did you say something, Jean-Pierre?

JEAN-PIERRE, *contemptuously.* Me? When?

MORIN. Mind your tongue, my friend! I'm warning you...

JEAN-PIERRE. And if not?

MORIN. If not?... You'll see! *(Aside.)* Damnable rebel! He'll bear watching, that one!... But patience! The least little misstep and I'll make him pay!

GALAOR, *to some of the blacks.* Come now... All of you who are working through the night... It's time. The sun is behind the coconut palms already.

MORIN. You heard him. Get a move on! *(They grumble and groan.)* As for the rest of you, there's still a half-hour of daylight work to do... *(The other group does likewise.)* But that's enough for today. No more until dawn... You're free to rest.

> *Surprised by his unexpected largesse, they voice various cries of joy: "Thank you!" "Oh, what a good master!" "Vive Morin!" etc.*

TÉLÉMAQUE. Bless you, master!

MORIN. Yes... I'm sure...

> *As* GALAOR *leads his muttering group off into the shed, the others celebrate their leisure; some with food, some with sleep, others with smoking, dancing, and general revelry.*

TÉLÉMAQUE. Who wants to have a tug-of-war?

JEAN-PIERRE, *aside.* Simple soul!

TÉLÉMAQUE, *holding out a length of rope.* Just you and me...

JEAN-PIERRE. Of course! *(Sarcastically.)* I have nothing better to do!

TÉLÉMAQUE, *taking him seriously.* Ready?

JEAN-PIERRE. Please! *(Menacingly.)* Leave me alone, or I'll—

TÉLÉMAQUE, *taken aback.* Oh!

He steps aside.

JUAN, *to* TÉLÉMAQUE. What did he do?

TÉLÉMAQUE. Nothing. He doesn't want to play. *(Holding out the rope.)* And you, Juan, *mi amigo*?

JUAN. Why not?

> *He takes the rope and the two begin tugging, continuing for a time.*

JEAN-PIERRE, *crossing down right, to* HÉLÈNE. Out of my way, viper!

HÉLÈNE. My God!

CLOTILDE, *to* VÉNUS. Did you hear that?

VÉNUS. What?

CLOTILDE. What he just called Hélène!

HERMIONE, *to* VÉNUS *and* CLOTILDE, *whispering.* What do you ex-pect? He and Timur were such good friends.

JEAN-PIERRE, *overhearing.* Who said that? Who mentioned Timur's name?

CLOTILDE, *pointing to* HERMIONE. She did.

JEAN-PIERRE, *to* HERMIONE, *suspiciously.* Do you know where he is?

HERMIONE. Heavens, no!

JEAN-PIERRE. Just as well! If any one of you knows, she'd best bite her tongue... Unless she wants to go play with the sharks, my friends!

HÉLÈNE, *to* JEAN-PIERRE, *timidly.* And you? Do you—

JEAN-PIERRE, *angrily interrupting.* Shut your mouth, slut!

As the women wince, he lies down on the ground, down right, while HÉLÈNE, *preoccupied, stands musing, down left. Both are apart from the others, who continue their various revels, growing more and more spirited...*

HERMIONE, *to* CLOTILDE. Look... The stars are out already... Did you know that the stars are the good Lord's eyes, Clotilde?

VÉNUS. Bah! What kind of nonsense...

HERMIONE. It's not nonsense! It's what the *bon père* told Galaor the other day.

CLOTILDE. Impossible! And I should know! I've seen him so many times, I have...

HERMIONE. You? You've seen God?

CLOTILDE. Yes. On the coast... We had one in our hut, made of ebony wood.

VÉNUS. Don't be such fools, you two! (*To* CLOTILDE.) How can the good Lord be made of wood? He would get all wormy! (*To* HERMIONE.) And if the stars were his eyes, why would he open them at night, when there's nothing to see?

HERMIONE. I guess... I never thought...

VÉNUS. How can you be so dumb? Don't you know that the good Lord is all flesh and blood, like a man, only bigger, and prettier, and with a long beard... (*To the men, cavorting about, pointing.*) Not like you ugly fools! (*To* HERMIONE *and* CLOTILDE.) Come, you two. That's enough for one day. It's time to put away our things.

TÉLÉMAQUE, *approaching as the three continue chatting amongst themselves, to* HÉLÈNE. You look sad. Wouldn't you like me to cheer you up?

HÉLÈNE. How, Télémaque?

TÉLÉMAQUE. I could talk to you about the carpenter.

HÉLÈNE, *eagerly.* About Timur?

TÉLÉMAQUE. I have news.

HÉLÈNE. Oh, yes! Tell me... Please!

TÉLÉMAQUE. Jean-Pierre saw him.

HÉLÈNE. Where? Where did he see him?

TÉLÉMAQUE. In the woods, with the runaways... He told us all about it. That is, he told his friends, not me. But I was there. I heard... He said that the carpenter was angry as could be. Fit to be tied, and that he was cursing... And that they were talking about you... And they called you a snake in the grass... But Jean-Pierre said that he wasn't going to tell you that he saw him because it would make you happy, and he didn't want to talk to you.

HÉLÈNE, *sighing.* Oh! I deserve it! But... It's not my fault. I'm not to blame.

TÉLÉMAQUE. Of course not!

HÉLÈNE. Please, Télémaque... Dear, dear Télémaque... What else did he say? Try to remember.

TÉLÉMAQUE. I didn't understand too much of the rest. Just that everything had to be secret... But that when Timur comes back, everything is going to be fine.

HÉLÈNE. "When Timur comes back..." Heaven help him, my friend! If he comes back they'll kill him!

TÉLÉMAQUE. Oh no... Jean-Pierre kept saying that everything will be over... That we... That everything is going to be fine. I didn't understand exactly, but I know that's what he said... That everything is going to be fine...

LÉON *appears stealthily, on the path, down left, standing in the shadows, gazing at* HÉLÈNE.

HÉLÈNE, *to herself.* How can it be? I don't know what to think...

TÉLÉMAQUE, *continuing.* That's all I remember.

HÉLÈNE, *to herself.* If he comes back... Oh! If only I could see him! But... I would be so afraid!

TÉLÉMAQUE, *continuing.* But they mustn't know I told you! They mustn't, you understand?

HÉLÈNE. Of course.

TÉLÉMAQUE *joins the other blacks, who are beginning to disperse, as* HÉLÈNE *joins* CLOTILDE, VÉNUS, *and* HERMIONE, *ambling left. She exits to her hut as the others exit down left, and as* JEAN-PIERRE *gets up from the ground.*

JEAN-PIERRE, *to* JUAN, *as they cross left.* It's getting late. It's time we went to bed, Juan. *(Pointing to the shed.)* Is Galaor on guard in there?

JUAN. Yes... He could be a problem...

JEAN-PIERRE. I know... I know.

JUAN. We'll have to be careful.

JEAN-PIERRE. So, is everything clear? We all get up when the moon is just over the belfry. They've been working since dawn, and by then they're all bound to be asleep! Even Galaor... Take my word!

JUAN. *Esperemos...* And you're sure he's coming?

JEAN-PIERRE. He promised... But who knows? *(As they are about to exit, down left, as an afterthought.)* And not a word to your wife!

JUAN. Trust me, Jean-Pierre!

> *They exit, up left, behind the last few blacks, leaving the stage empty. A moment later,* LÉON *cautiously steps out of the shadows.*

LÉON, *looking about.* No one... *(Looking toward the shed.)* Except in there, at the presses... Not dark enough yet... But I can't just wait and do nothing. *(Pacing uneasily, stopping from time to time.)* Wherever I look I see her! So beautiful... Ah! Those lovely bare shoulders... That glorious bosom... Oh! Why not? Why shouldn't I... Why resist? Why force myself when it would be so easy? *(Changing his mind, angrily.)* No!... Good God, how can I... They're slaves... Vulgar creatures, lowly brutes... Beasts that I've often whipped into submission! And I would take one of their vile kind to my bed? Make her my mistress? *(After a pause.)* Why not? Where's the shame? As long as no one knows... As long as the blacks have no idea... If they thought there was any similarity between us... Their passions and ours... *(With a wry little smile.)* Indeed! At this moment there's not much difference... Oh, I blush to think... Damn! Still, I wouldn't be the first. Is there any white on this island, any planter who hasn't... Who hasn't... Bah! A hundred times!... Even my father, I'm sure, when he was younger... And what's the harm? A pleasure that doesn't hurt anyone, after all... If it were evil, would Nature goad us into it the way she does? What good would all my philosophy be if it didn't rid me of such wrong-headed notions? Such prejudiced ideas... Man yearns to be happy. And as long as it's not at another's expense... *(Stopping left, by the entrance to* HÉLÈNE'S *hut, gazing at it.)* And with her? What difference could it possibly make? *(With a little laugh.)* Can I sully her reputation? Her honor? Her religious principles?... What principles? What honor? She has none, poor simple, primitive creature! None of civilized man's conventions!... She's a child of nature... Ah, Rousseau! Rousseau! How well you knew love and the human heart! How proud have I been to see myself stride through your passionate pages! When I think of Saint-Preux's letter in Julie's bedchamber, it's myself I see there![3] Musing, like him, on the pleasures of the flesh... Tasting in advance the happiness before me... Lusting after it in my mind... Ah! To see her in all her beauty, trembling there... A feast for the senses... That night, in the banana trees... Poor child, how she wept... But they all do. They weep because they know that our women weep! They're like apes, these blacks... They imitate all we do... Well, this time, I wager, she'll not put up a fight. *(Looking about.)* Black as pitch... Yes, it's time. This is her hut... Ah! I will! I'll go in... I... *(Excitedly.)* Yes, I... *(Suddenly, with a start, as he hears a crackling sound, softly.)* What? What's that?... Some-one... Who... ?

> *As he retreats cautiously, up right, and stands on edge,* TIMUR *appears at the top of the hill, up left, silhouetted for a moment against the night sky, then comes quickly downstage, stopping several times to look about.*

TIMUR, *not noticing* LÉON. No one... *(In front of* HÉLÈNE's *hut.)* Ah! Her hut... *(Suddenly noticing him, under his breath.)* Who...

LÉON, *under his breath.* A black!

TIMUR, *under his breath.* A white!... Damn! Then it must be... Ah!

> *He seizes the hatchet in his waistband and moves deliber-ately toward him.*

3. In *Julie; ou, La Nouvelle Héloïse,* an epistolary novel published by Rousseau in 1761, the tutor Saint-Preux falls in love with and seduces his student Julie d'Étanges, the daughter of a Swiss nobleman. Rémusat refers to Lettre 14 in the first part of the novel.

LÉON, *under his breath.* A lover, perhaps?... We'll see about that! *(Approaching him, aloud.)* You! What are you doing here?

TIMUR, *arrogantly.* And you?

LÉON. Me? Are you mad? How dare you question me! Do you know who I am, you scum?

TIMUR. Of course I do.

LÉON, *center.* Well? Explain yourself! What are you doing here? Do you know the time? *(Pointing right, to the shed.)* Why aren't you working? *(Pointing left.)* Or asleep in your quarters?... Or are you just out whoring... Chasing some woman, you miserable rabble! Back where you belong, before I—

TIMUR, *waving his hatchet.* Before you what? *(Controlling himself.)* No...

LÉON. Before I call the guard! Now leave!

> *The door to the shed opens, lighting the area around it, and* GALAOR, *attracted by the noise, appears.*

GALAOR, *right, sleepily.* What the devil... Who's there?

LÉON. I am, Galaor.

GALAOR, *peering.* Monsieur? The young master? But—

LÉON, *sarcastically.* One of your blacks decided to take a stroll.

GALAOR. Aha... No harm, monsieur... Their time is their own until the sun comes up.

LÉON. Yes... Of course...

GALAOR. Sleep well, master.

He returns and shuts the door.

LÉON. Damn! I've lost my chance... *(To* TIMUR, *still at* HÉLÈNE's *hut, resisting the obvious temptation to strike him.)* Now you! Leave, I told you!

He exits, down left, leaving TIMUR *alone.*

TIMUR. Bah! Let him go! When I kill him I want to be sure he knows why! *(Pacing.)* Ah! If only she were here... Yes, I would have slit her... *(emphasizing)* ...her master's throat and flung his head into her lap! Well, patience! Patience!... The great day will come. I'm glad I held my temper. It's not enough to kill him. I need more, much more... They would have caught me, hauled me off. And that would have been that!... Jean-Pierre has spread the word, I'm sure. Tonight is the night... They're waiting for me... *(He looks about in disgust.)* Vile hole! *(Apostrophizing the surroundings.)* So! We meet again! When I left, who thought I would be coming back so soon? And with such high hopes! Jean-Pierre says they're ready. Well, we'll see... The whip and irons can change a lot of minds... And days and nights of work, work, work!... Especially these Creoles... Not like us Africans, I'm afraid... When I tried to explain my plan, most of them didn't understand. The others agreed it was a good idea... But help me? Not a one!... No matter. The plan is sound... It can't fail. I've worked over it too long to let it fail now... Why not? We have strong arms, like them. Even stronger!... We do all the work that's too hard for them, good God! We have eyes to see with and mouths to shout with... And courage... Ah! I remember Cayor,[4] and how we hunted lions... *(He muses silently for a few moments, nodding.)*

---

4. Cayor was the most powerful and important kingdom to secede from the Jolof empire in the sixteenth century. It was located in north-central Senegal.

There are twenty of us for every one of them. And it's our own fault, by God! They're the ones who are prisoners... *Our* prisoners, *our* slaves, *our* dogs!... Oh yes! My plan is sound. But we let ourselves be shackled and beaten. No rest, no pleasure, nothing to call our own... Not a thing... They measure out our food, they begrudge us our tobacco, forbid us our whiskey! Far from our mothers, our brothers... They even take our women... Yes, our women... Ah! Badia... Badia... They took your name... But you gave him your body! He didn't even force you!... His, bought and paid for!... And not for one moment did you remember your poor Touko! *(Sighing.)* Ah! When the ship came and carried you off from the coast, what did I do, Badia? For three days and three nights I stood on the burning sand, too desperate even to eat! Then, at dusk each day, I would come to the shore... To look at the sea where the ship had long since disappeared in the distance... I would look for some trace of you left on the waves... In vain... In vain... And when, two years later, a slave merchant bought me, my only hope, as they bound me in chains... My only hope in that foul marketplace was to think that, at least, I was heading to the west... The west, where my Badia was... And when I found you... You, my long-lost love... You said I was in your every thought, and you took me in your arms, clasped me to your breast... Oh, how happy I was! I almost felt free... Free, and back in our African home... *(He pauses, then continues, cynically.)* And all that... Ah! All that... For what? Only to be betrayed! Only so she could go off with that cursèd white!... Yes, I saw them... Saw them with my own eyes... I followed them to the banana trees. But the trees were too thick... They disappeared... I ran everywhere, I looked... And then I found the spot. The place where they had been... I saw the grass, all matted down, and the leaves on the ground, all crushed and crumbled... And my blood... *(Passionately.)* Oh! How it boiled within me!... No! *(Pounding his chest, deter-*

mined.) No quarter! No mercy! None of them will be spared! Not a one! And nothing... Not a thing... Not a stone, not a tree!... And you, white villain! I'll tie you to a tree, and I'll go find your sister, and you'll watch her do what my Badia did... Only then will I kill you! *(In a rage.)* Yes, kill you, in front of Badia herself! And I'll make her drink your blood, and... Oh, wicked Badia! Oh, wicked Hélène!... Then poor Touko can die in peace.

As he withdraws slowly, up center, JEAN-PIERRE *enters cautiously, up left, beckoning to other blacks, who follow him.*

JEAN-PIERRE. Shhh... Shhh...

The ensuing exchanges are spoken in whispers.

TIMUR, *up center.* Who goes?

JEAN-PIERRE. Timur?

TIMUR. Ah! Jean-Pierre! It's you...

JEAN-PIERRE, *motioning to the others.* Come... It's the carpenter... *(To* TIMUR, *embracing him.)* My friend... My friend... *(As the others approach, up center.)* We weren't sure... We heard a noise... We were afraid...

TIMUR. No need... It's safe...

The group huddles about the two men.

JUAN, *to* TIMUR. How good to see you!

TÉLÉMAQUE. Is that Timur and not a ghost?

TIMUR. I assure you, Télémaque...

TÉLÉMAQUE. And is it true that you're in the mountains, with the runaways?

TIMUR. Yes... It's true...

TÉLÉMAQUE. And that you run through the countryside, free as you please? All by yourself?

TIMUR. Do you worry about me, friend?

TÉLÉMAQUE. But the island is so big! Me, I would get lost! I wouldn't be able—

TIMUR, *cutting him off.* Enough! We're wasting precious time, comrades. Did Jean-Pierre tell you what we're doing?

JUAN. He told us that he went to cut down trees in the forest...

TÉLÉMAQUE. That he stopped for a moment to kill a bird...

TIMUR, *impatiently.* Yes, yes... Did he tell you...

JUAN. And that he saw you there... That you told him you were free now...

TÉLÉMAQUE. Free, Timur!

JUAN. Free and happy... And that you wanted us to be free as well... That you said it would make us happy too!... That's what he told us. So now we're ready to escape, like you. To run away...

JEAN-PIERRE. Run away? But... (*To* TIMUR.) That's not what I said! (*To the others.*) It's not!

TIMUR. No! Not run away... Do you want to spend the rest of your lives in the mountains? Hunted down like wild beasts? Shot at like pigeons?... No, you want something better! You want to count yourselves, and count your enemies... And then—

TÉLÉMAQUE. Enemies?

The others echo his question, mumbling: "Enemies?"
"What enemies?" "Who do you mean?" etc.

TIMUR. What enemies? By God! Your masters, that's who!

ALMANZOR, *one of the group.* The whites!

TIMUR. Is it so hard to understand? Are they so strong and clever
that they can't be attacked? Don't they ever fall asleep? Can't
you ever surprise them?

TÉLÉMAQUE, *naïvely.* To do what?

TIMUR. Do what? Do—

JEAN-PIERRE. To kill them, good God!

ALMANZOR. Yes! We'll stuff them in the presses... Like poor old Roger.

The others voice their agreement: "Yes, yes!" "The presses!"
"That's what we'll do!" etc.

TÉLÉMAQUE. And after that we'll go ask the master for a drink.

JEAN-PIERRE. What master? There won't be any master!

TÉLÉMAQUE. Not this one... Another one...

TIMUR. What other one? We'll be free, I tell you!

ALMANZOR. Free? How?

TIMUR. Don't you understand? We're going to revolt! We're going
to have a rebellion!

The others respond with muttered, disbelieving questions:
"Revolt?" "Rebellion?" "What did he say?" etc.

JEAN-PIERRE. Yes! You know what that means?

TÉLÉMAQUE. But they'll hang us!

ALMANZOR. Or hamstring us at least!

TIMUR. But they won't! We'll be the masters!...

TÉLÉMAQUE. We will? And I'll have my whiskey?

TIMUR, *continuing*. Our own masters!...

ALMANZOR, *to himself*. What masters? Who will be our slaves?

TIMUR, *continuing*. Our own masters! Masters of the ground beneath our feet! Of the air we breathe! We won't live for someone else... Like a tool that wears out and gets sold, second-hand... Sold like a barrel of sugar, my friends!

JEAN-PIERRE, *to* TIMUR. Tell them that the runaways have promised to help us.

TIMUR, *to the others*. You heard what he said. The runaways will help free you.

ALMANZOR. Then why bother? If they're going to free us, why should we take the trouble to revolt?

TIMUR, *becoming frustrated*. Why should you... No, no! They can only help! Only you can free yourselves. If the runaways showed their faces on the plantations... Armed to the teeth... The garrison would hear and shoot them dead in their tracks! What would you do in the forest with all your freedom? What good would it do you?... No, no... It's here, on the plantation, that you have to rise up...

ALMANZOR. Rise up?

TIMUR. But not all alone... That would be madness... My plan is to work with the other plantations. Twenty of them, here and there, on the island... There are free blacks all over. I know... I've been

told... At Cap-Français and Port-au-Prince...[5] Even whites who
are on our side...

ALMANZOR. There are?

TIMUR. Working for us...

TÉLÉMAQUE, *incredulous.* No!

TIMUR. The revolt will break out everywhere, all at once. It will
spread like wildfire, swift as a winter hurricane, swallowing
everything in its path... It will sweep away plantations, houses,
dead bodies... Saint-Domingue will be ours! Our land!

JEAN-PIERRE, *exclaiming.* Fire and blood!

> *All the blacks, except* TÉLÉMAQUE, JUAN, *and* ALMANZOR,
> *echo his exclamations.*

TIMUR. Our new Africa!

> *The same blacks repeat, "Our new Africa! Our new Africa!"*

JEAN-PIERRE, *as the cries subside.* So, when do we begin?

ALMANZOR. We don't want to begin.

JEAN-PIERRE. What?

ALMANZOR, *pointing up left, toward the hill.* Let the ones up there
begin. Then we'll see...

TIMUR. What? You poor wretches! Somebody has to lead the dance!
Don't you understand?

TÉLÉMAQUE. Dance? Why—

5. Today the capital, Port-au-Prince is located on the north coast of Haiti, west
of Le Cap.

JEAN-PIERRE. Idiot! (*To* TIMUR.) You'll have rifles for us, won't you?

TIMUR. Yes, the runaways promise... Besides, how many will you need? Three or four good shots, and you're rid of your masters!

ALMANZOR. So you say. But you're free. With us, the steward is always on our backs. Better go ahead without us.

Several blacks echo: "Yes, without us!" "He's right!" etc.

TIMUR, *angrily.* You... Oh! You fools! You timid, lily-livered... *(Choking with indignation.)* You were born to serve, to sleep, and to die! You could have been the bison, leaping through the savannas, or plunging into the rivers! Instead, what are you? The ox, who labors until he drops, who grazes in the stable and feeds with his flesh the one who struck him down! That's what they've made you!... What good are your backs? Only to haul a load! Your arms? Only to swing a pick! Your shoulders? Only to feel the bite of the lash!... So be it! Keep your shackles! Hand them down to your children, to your African brothers, who, thanks to you, will keep coming, age after age, to recruit you like a flock that the plague has devastated!... God help us! When my chief... *(emphasizing)* ...my chief himself sold me to some brigand from Europe, and my neck was locked in an iron collar...[6] When they laid me on the ground, on a foul plank, chained to thirty comrades, with my legs curled up beneath me... When, in that unspeakable pit, condemned to its stifling stench for forty days and nights, unable to move, surrounded by the bodies of the sick and the dying, deafened by their pathetic cries... When I even began to see slavery as a deliverance... Oh, how I would dream of the brothers I was about to meet... The brothers who seemed to be waiting for me to help

6. It is widely acknowledged today that African tribal leaders often were complicitous with European slave traders.

them wreak their vengeance! Yes, the one pleasure of my torment, its one and only charm, was the hope of one day killing our murderers! *(After a pause, ironically.)* Ah! Why can I not still be lying in that suffocating dungeon! At least I could still have hope... I could still dream of the freedom of my brothers... Their courage, their will, their determination!...

TÉLÉMAQUE. But...

ALMANZOR. But...

JUAN. Please, Timur...

TIMUR, *ignoring them, continuing.* I would not know the agony of learning, to my shame, that my comrades in misery are amused by what makes me suffer in their midst... Pleased by what costs me my life... And to see that they have lost not only their homeland but even their very hearts! *(To the blacks.)* O woe, you unworthy... What have you done? How can it be that I loathe the white man less!

JEAN-PIERRE, *to* TIMUR, *as the group mutters its reaction to his tirade.* Please, my friend... They are with us, I assure you!... Almanzor?... Juan?

JUAN. Yes, yes!... Just give me a rifle...

ALMANZOR. And me...

TÉLÉMAQUE. If there's an uprising, I'm with you.

> The others echo with shouts of "So am I!" "Me too!" "I'm with you!" etc.

TIMUR. You'll have your rifles... All of you... And there *will* be an uprising, my friends. You can count on it!

ALMANZOR. Where?

TÉLÉMAQUE. Where will we have to go?

JEAN-PIERRE. Into our enemies' bellies, that's where!

TÉLÉMAQUE, *to himself.* Their bellies?

TIMUR. Come... It's growing late. Best we all leave... Be ready for tomorrow. I'll come earlier. At dusk... Work is stopping for a time, I'm told...

JEAN-PIERRE. Oh?

TIMUR. Yes... In the afternoon.

JEAN-PIERRE. How do you know?

TIMUR. No matter... I know!... Now listen to me. Someone is coming here tomorrow. A white... From France...

> *The blacks mutter their surprise: "From France?" "A white?" etc.*

JEAN-PIERRE. What?

TIMUR, *continuing.* Treat him well, you hear? He's one of us...

ALMANZOR, *puzzled.* He is?

TÉLÉMAQUE. A white?

TIMUR. Not "one of us," but on our side...[7] And no one must know. Make sure your friends are with you, but not a word, you hear? Let them expect anything... When they hear the cry: "Africa and freedom!"...

ALMANZOR *and* JUAN. Africa and freedom!

---

7. The French abolitionist Société des Amis des Noirs was created in February 1788.

The others enthusiastically repeat the cry.

TIMUR. Shhh!... Farewell, my friends... *(To* JEAN-PIERRE, *softly.)* Can we count on them, Jean-Pierre?

JEAN-PIERRE, *with a note of doubt.* I wonder... I wonder...

TIMUR. No matter... We're on our way. There's no turning back. Besides, others will do better!

JEAN-PIERRE. Africa and freedom!

TIMUR. Africa and freedom! *(They embrace.)* Farewell, brother.

JEAN-PIERRE. Farewell...

TIMUR. Africa... *(As he exits up the hill, up left.)* And freedom!

JEAN-PIERRE *stands for a moment, watches him go, then exits, up left.*

End of Act II

ACT III

Same set as in Act II.

At rise, Morin, down center, is talking with César Julien, a mulatto, who is holding a shotgun. Other blacks pass back and forth from time to time.

CÉSAR JULIEN. What a brilliant idea, I must say! To come here this morning, while I was out hunting...

MORIN. Oh?

CÉSAR JULIEN. ...and see that deputy from the Assemblée. The one who's spending the day with the Valombres... What a pleasure it's going to be to meet him!

MORIN. Maybe for you... Frankly, I have no stomach for those windbags from the Continent, who honor us with their presence... Who don't know sugarcane from bamboo, and who turn everything topsy-turvy in the presses...

CÉSAR JULIEN. But he's not here to see the presses. *(Pointing right.)* They're running just fine! He's here for other, more important matters.

MORIN. More important? Well, I can't stand these busybodies who poke their noses into my business. The blacks give us enough trouble, thank you! I don't need someone to come add to it with more rules and regulations, and all kinds of damnable problems!

CÉSAR JULIEN. Come, come, my friend. The questions the Colonial Constitution[1] is bringing up at the moment are certainly not unreasonable. And questions that the motherland has to address, in its fatherly wisdom!... *(He smiles at his bon mot.)* Present conditions are in need of reform. Surely you'll not deny—

MORIN, *interrupting.* True enough... Monsieur de Valombre tells me time and again that we have to take care not to let the mulattoes elbow their way into the running of the colony.

CÉSAR JULIEN, *taken aback.* Oh? He tells you—

MORIN, *with a shrug.* But then...

CÉSAR JULIEN. I must say, that doesn't sound like him, my friend. His views are usually so enlightened, so... *(looking for a word)* ...so philanthropistic...

MORIN, *nodding, without conviction.* Of course... Of course...

CÉSAR JULIEN. None of those small-minded prejudices of color!

MORIN. No... No...

CÉSAR JULIEN. I mean, what difference can the shade of one's skin make to those natural rights conferred on us at birth? How can one refuse a political life to educated men like us, I ask you?

MORIN. Us?

CÉSAR JULIEN. It's a disgrace!

MORIN. And you think that the deputy is here to change all that?

---

1. There was no constitution in Saint-Domingue prior to 1801. The author perhaps seeks here to call attention to the character's faulty understanding of the events occurring around him.

CÉSAR JULIEN. Can you doubt it? A man with his experience, his knowledge... Why else would he be here? The present regime is quite intolerable for our kind... *(As* MORIN *stares up in the air, down left, over the footlights.)* I say, what are you looking at?

MORIN, *pointing in the air, down left, following with his finger.* You see that flamingo?

CÉSAR JULIEN. Ah! Wait... *(Aiming his shotgun.)* Let me get it...

MORIN. Don't waste your fire. It's off too far. You'll never—

CÉSAR JULIEN. You think so, do you? This gun may be small, but even thirty feet farther...

MORIN. Bah!

CÉSAR JULIEN. Would you like to bet? Two *gourdes*² and a glass of cherry brandy!

MORIN. Forget it...

CÉSAR JULIEN, *pointing down right, over the footlights.* You see that black?³ The one over there, picking sweet potatoes? I bet I can hit him right between the shoulders.

        He takes aim.

MORIN, *pushing the gun aside.* Careful with that! If you wound him he'll have an excuse not to work. And at a busy time like this...

CÉSAR JULIEN. Don't worry. It's only buckshot. *(Shooting.)* Fire!

MORIN, *with a laugh.* He didn't even turn around!

2. A *gourde* is the basic unit of money in Haiti.
3. Persons of color were slow to recognize common political cause with black slaves. Some were themselves slave owners.

CÉSAR JULIEN. Goddamn! His hide must be made of leather! I have a charge in the other barrel. Let me show you...

MORIN. Don't bother!... You're lucky to have so much time to go hunting. I wish I could!

CÉSAR JULIEN. Who's stopping you?

MORIN. Ha! If only... With all the slaves to look after? I'm almost a slave myself!

CÉSAR JULIEN. Tsk tsk tsk!

MORIN, *hearing a noise coming from the house, down left, beyond the footlights.* What's that? Is the deputy here already?

CÉSAR JULIEN, *peering.* I think... Yes, by the door... I can see them through the panes. Monsieur de Valombre and Madame...

MORIN. Then it must be the deputy. Monsieur told me to make sure all the blacks are at their places. He wants to show him how well run we are. The presses and all...

CÉSAR JULIEN, *looking down left.* Here they come... If you'll excuse me... I'll go and join the group.

> *He puts his gun down against a tree and prepares to come downstage, with exaggerated affectation.* VALOMBRE *and* DE TENDALE *enter, down left, followed by* MADAME DE VALOMBRE, *fanning herself,* LÉON, *and* CÉLESTINE.

VALOMBRE, *to* DE TENDALE. Yes, monsieur. As you can see, the plantation house is especially well situated. *(Pointing down right.)* On that side, a lovely garden, bordering the fields... *(Pointing down left.)* And behind it, the ocean... *(Pointing upstage.)* And the mountains, monsieur...

DE TENDALE, *very pompously.* A most picturesque prospect! One might say it is nature embellished by man's labor!

VALOMBRE. Indeed!... Of course, our garden cannot be compared to your parks, monsieur. We are obliged to till most of it for our personal use.

DE TENDALE. Ah! So much the better! How much more to be preferred is this happy, productive plot of land, whose view would bring joy to the philosopher of wealth,[4] than those majestically sterile gardens of ours, true emblem of the aristocracy that planted them!

LÉON, *aside to* VALOMBRE. You see, papá?

VALOMBRE, *to* DE TENDALE. Too kind, monsieur. *(Noticing* CÉSAR JULIEN, *who has been waiting impatiently to be introduced.)* Ah! César...

CÉSAR JULIEN. Monsieur de Valombre... May I present my respects... *(To* MADAME DE VALOMBRE.) And is your daughter well, madame?

MADAME DE VALOMBRE, *as* DE TENDALE *ignores him.* Rather, monsieur... Though she does have the vapors...

CÉLESTINE, *aside to* MADAME DE VALOMBRE. I do, mammá?

DE TENDALE, *to* VALOMBRE, *gazing about, admiringly.* I could contemplate this view endlessly, monsieur. *(To* MADAME DE VALOMBRE.) How this lovely locale must delight you, madame! *(With a wave of the hand.)* Greenery, abundant blooms... So much good to spread round... The true homeland of mademoiselle, your charming daughter... The very ideal of innocence and well-being...

CÉSAR JULIEN *continues to stand uneasily, waiting.*

---

4. The French physiocrats of the second half of the eighteenth century held that agriculture was the primary source of a nation's wealth.

MADAME DE VALOMBRE, *fanning herself.* Yes... Though the irrigation ditches do make it rather humid...

DE TENDALE. Oh?

MADAME DE VALOMBRE. And in the evening one's lungs tend to become quite congested.

DE TENDALE, *ignoring her remark, to* LÉON. And you, my young friend... How grateful I am for your kind invitation to meet your estimable family! It's clear to me how you come by your virtuous sentiments... Your humane ideas...

VALOMBRE. Ah yes! My son does have ideas, thank heaven! I have made him read, monsieur. All your philosophers... Voltaire, Rousseau, Marmontel...[5]

DE TENDALE. The preceptors and mentors of the human race! Yes! Their lessons have taken root and sprouted in that young head of his!

MADAME DE VALOMBRE, *to* VALOMBRE. Perhaps monsieur would like to rest a bit before you show him round.

VALOMBRE. Of course! (*To* DE TENDALE.) What was I thinking? You must be tired. Fatigued... Considering how far you have come!

He chuckles.

DE TENDALE. Not at all, monsieur. I forgot the distance when I considered the goal! "Beyond that ocean," I kept telling myself, "there are men—miserable, oppressed, degraded creatures—upon whom I am bequeathing the benefits of our French Revolution..."

---

5. Jean-François Marmontel, the author of *Les Incas; ou, La Destruction de l'empire du Pérou* (1777), placed fanaticism and violence in a global context and argued for liberal colonizing practices.

VALOMBRE, *unenthusiastically.* Indeed...

DE TENDALE. How could I complain of the rigors of my travels when I, monsieur, was the emissary, the missionary of humanity!

CÉSAR JULIEN, *to* VALOMBRE. Excuse me, monsieur, but... Might I...

VALOMBRE. César?

CÉSAR JULIEN. Would you be so good as to introduce me?

VALOMBRE. Of course, *mon cher. (To* DE TENDALE.) Monsieur de Tendale, permit me to present César Julien. *(Almost apologetically.)* A person of color... A mulatto... But we think no less of him for it, I assure you. Because... Because we have principles...

we're not predjuice

DE TENDALE, *shaking* CÉSAR JULIEN's *hand.* Charmed, monsieur! What a delight to make the acquaintance of one who belongs to such an interesting social class!

CÉSAR JULIEN. Monsieur, your arrival has been awaited with the greatest impatience. It has raised the hopes of certain ones amongst us. You can hardly imagine...

DE TENDALE. And I trust I may fulfill them! That is my most ardent wish. Oh, obstacles there shall be aplenty. But together we shall overcome them. When one stands surrounded by patriots of such enlightened stripe, can one doubt the success of our sublime cause? Ought one despair?

VALOMBRE, *still unenthusiastically.* Indeed...

DE TENDALE, *continuing.* The truth, monsieur, is like the sun. It shines its light on both worlds, old and new.

LÉON, *to* DE TENDALE. Monsieur, my father dares not ask if you would like to visit our presses. I agree that it is not an imposing or philosophical sight, but surely there is interest in whatever one observes.

DE TENDALE. Certainly, my young friend! And what a sight it must be! Not "imposing or philosophical"? I beg to differ! What greater spectacle than to watch production *in processu*? To catch it in the act, so to speak! To penetrate to society's very heart, its very soul, in the bosom of the impoverished, the useful laboring class... What more imposing sight? Labor and the people!

VALOMBRE. Yes... Yes...

DE TENDALE, *continuing.* And why do we do as we do, if not for them? Those laborers, those workers? In a word, the people... Disdained for so long... Your thunderous presses, your fertile fields... Ah, my young friend... Such is "the palace of the people's majesty," to borrow a phrase from the great Mirabeau.[6]

LÉON. Yes, monsieur. All that is most admirable in France. But here in the colonies... We have no "people," as you call them.[7] We have blacks, monsieur... Slaves...

DE TENDALE, *nodding.* And an interesting social class they are!

CÉSAR JULIEN, *aside.* "Interesting"? Blacks?

DE TENDALE, *continuing.* All the more interesting since their enslavement is undeserved...

CÉSAR JULIEN, *continuing aside.* He calls *them* "interesting" too?

DE TENDALE, *continuing.* ...and their fate most intolerable!

VALOMBRE, *to* LÉON, *in a whisper.* Your philosopher is getting carried away.

---

6. A leading figure in the French Revolution, Mirabeau was a moderate who, like Rémusat, favored an English-style constitutional monarchy.

7. In his celebrated analysis of the Haitian revolution, *The Black Jacobins,* C. L. R. James compares the three main groups in France based on class (aristocracy, middle class, people) to those based on race in Saint-Domingue (whites, persons of color, blacks).

LÉON, *replying, in a whisper.* Reason will do that, papá. *(To* DE TEN-
DALE, *aloud.)* Shall we begin our rounds, monsieur? You shall
see for yourself. What better way to observe, after all? Experience is the only path to truth.

DE TENDALE. Experience and study! I see that our young patriot
has learned his lessons well.

LÉON. Thank you, monsieur. I have read a bit of Condillac...[8]

DE TENDALE. Ah yes... Condillac! A well-formed mind and great
clarity of spirit. But no fire in his belly! *(With a self-conscious
little look toward the two women.)* If I may be so bold... He cannot hold a candle to our Rousseau, do you not agree?

LÉON. I do, indeed... *(Calling to his servant.)* Jean-Jacques! Jean-
Jacques!

DE TENDALE, *misunderstanding.* Ah! What a joy to hear you invoke
his name with such energy of youth, such passion...

LÉON, *to himself.* That damnable... Where on earth...

        JEAN-JACQUES, *a black, appears, down left.*

JEAN-JACQUES, *to* LÉON. Monsieur called?

LÉON. I did indeed! And I'll thank you not to dawdle when I call you.

JEAN-JACQUES. Very good, monsieur.

LÉON. Now go bring us some parasols, Jean-Jacques!

DE TENDALE, *taken aback.* Oh?

8. Étienne Bonnot de Condillac was an eighteenth-century French philosopher
and Enlightenment figure. As the discussion here indicates, Condillac's psycho-
logical theory of empirical sensationism posits that knowledge is obtained through
experience.

JEAN-JACQUES. Yes, monsieur.

He exits, down left.

LÉON, *to* DE TENDALE. He's my black, monsieur. I named him after the immortal author of *The Social Contract.*[9]

DE TENDALE. Yes... I see... Well then, shall we be off, messieurs? I am eager to watch these gentle blacks at their labors. *(To himself.)* At last, to see these timeless victims of prejudice and oppression... My mission is about to begin. *(To* VALOMBRE, LÉON, *and* CÉSAR JULIEN.*)* Messieurs...

JEAN-JACQUES *enters hurriedly, down left, with a parasol for each of the four men, who exit along the path, down right, with* VALOMBRE *and* LÉON *in the lead.* MORIN *follows at a distance, without a parasol.*

CÉLESTINE, *to* MADAME DE VALOMBRE, *coming down left.* I don't know what it is, mammá, but that gentleman has the oddest way of talking. He sounds as if he's reading from a book.

MADAME DE VALOMBRE. That's how intelligent people in Paris talk, love.

CÉLESTINE. But mammá... Really... I saw so many intelligent people! And not a one of them talked like that. Just the opposite, in fact... People said it was good taste to talk simply.

MADAME DE VALOMBRE. Heavens, child! What do you expect? Since the Revolution... *(Looking about.)* Goodness! Do you feel that breeze?

9. *The Social Contract* is a work of political philosophy by Rousseau, published in 1762. Especially relevant to Rémusat's play is the centrality for Rousseau of the general will of the people.

CÉLESTINE. Yes... And a good thing, too. It's so dreadfully hot...

MADAME DE VALOMBRE. Be a dear and tell Marie-Louise to bring us two chairs.

CÉLESTINE. Yes, mammá.

She exits, down left, leaving MADAME DE VALOMBRE *alone, fanning herself. A moment later,* CÉLESTINE *returns, down left, followed shortly by* MARIE-LOUISE, *carrying two chairs.*

MADAME DE VALOMBRE, *to* MARIE-LOUISE. Ah, there you are...

MARIE-LOUISE. Yes, madame.

She sets down the chairs and exits. The two women sit down.

CÉLESTINE. You know, mammá... I do wish I could read something by that Monsieur Rousseau. The one they were talking about... The one my brother likes so much... I heard his name all the time in Paris, but my aunt kept saying that he wasn't for children... That I was too young...

MADAME DE VALOMBRE. Aha!... Well... I've been looking for something to give you to read. Why not him? You can read me a dozen pages every night. Aloud... While your father plays chess...

CÉLESTINE, *clapping.* And what will we read?

MADAME DE VALOMBRE. We'll see. You can ask your brother for something. He can lend us that book he was mentioning just now.

CÉLESTINE. *The Social Contract?*

MADAME DE VALOMBRE. Yes. That should be good for a young lady. It's not a novel.

CÉLESTINE, *looking down right, toward the path.* Oh mammá! Here he comes now. *(Pointing.)* You see? And he's all alone.

MADAME DE VALOMBRE. My, my... Did something happen to him, I wonder? *(To herself.)* Children, children! They never give us a moment's peace!

LÉON *enters.*

CÉLESTINE, *standing.* Brother dear... You've left the others?

LÉON, *with a careless little wave.* Yes...

MADAME DE VALOMBRE. Is something wrong, Léon?

LÉON. What could be wrong, mammá?

MADAME DE VALOMBRE. I don't know. It's just that... You're coming back all alone, and—

CÉLESTINE. It's very strange.

LÉON. No... I assure you...

CÉLESTINE. But you were in such a hurry to show our guest the plantation.

LÉON. Papá is with him.

CÉLESTINE. Tell me the truth, Léon. Aren't you a little unhappy with him? A trifle less impressed than you were?

LÉON. No...

CÉLESTINE. Just yesterday morning, I mean...

LÉON. Not at all! He's a brilliant gentleman. Well-informed... With a most enlightened spirit of the times... A philosopher, Célestine...

CÉLESTINE. But you do seem a little less attracted by his enlightened spirit, brother dear.

LÉON. A little, perhaps... But you have to understand. These gentlemen from France are very quick to judge things that they don't know at all. Once they know the facts... Once they see for themselves... Men like Monsieur de Tendale...

He pauses.

CÉLESTINE. Yes?

LÉON. With his principles... That is... He judges the affairs of our plantation like a blind man. He's very strong in his theories, but in practice, I'm afraid...

CÉLESTINE. What did he say?

LÉON. My goodness! Nothing definite... But he uses certain expressions... Certain gestures, sister dear... Things that are simply improper in front of blacks at the presses...

CÉLESTINE. Oh?

LÉON. He treats them like equals. For example, he asked them if they were happy with their lives. He asked one if he was married. He passed by one whose collar had left a scar... A very small scar... And he asked how it happened. When they told him, his jaw dropped and he gave the black some coins! Money, you hear?... You know how I try to keep order... Discipline... I did my best once or twice to tell him. To explain... But he didn't seem to understand... I don't like to argue, especially with a gentleman whose principles I respect and share! So I left...

MADAME DE VALOMBRE, *still seated, fanning.* I say, son! That *is* unpleasant! Who asked him to come here and disrupt our life? Why couldn't he leave us alone, with his revolution?

CÉLESTINE. What can I say? (*To* LÉON.) I'm afraid you're going to have to choose between your principles, on the one hand, and our plantation, on the other.

LÉON. Not at all! Principles are principles! They're always true. And a clever mind knows how to put them into practice. Experience, Célestine!... When Monsieur de Tendale has spent a week here with us, he'll know much more, and he'll feel just as we do.

CÉLESTINE. But won't he be less of a philosopher then?

    She sits down.

LÉON. Nonsense! Philosophy is philosophy, and business is business!

    VALOMBRE, DE TENDALE, *and* CÉSAR JULIEN *enter, down right.* MORIN *follows at a respectable distance.* CÉLESTINE *stands up as soon as* DE TENDALE *appears, and stands by* MADAME DE VALOMBRE, *still seated, fanning.*

DE TENDALE, *to* VALOMBRE. At least, monsieur, if you would be good enough to relieve them of their labors for the rest of the day... I should like to observe them in all their daily occupations. Recreation as well as work...

VALOMBRE. Perfectly reasonable, monsieur... That's the least... (*To* MORIN.) You hear, Morin? (MORIN *nods, grudgingly, and exits, down left.*) But as for your other suggestions, monsieur... I'm afraid I must decline. Do away with the rod? The whip?... Really, I might as well plant the sugarcane myself!

DE TENDALE. Indeed, monsieur! I find such an objection from so enlightened a humanitarian as yourself rather shocking. (*To* LÉON.) My dear Léon... If I may say, your father reasons ill. I entrust you with the task of bringing his principles into harmony with our century... Yours and mine!

LÉON. Monsieur... My father is accustomed to the working of the plantation. Whereas you—

DE TENDALE. Quite! Accustomed to his habits... And he wants to cling to them, I see. I find that unfortunate. But you, my young friend... You, who are conversant with our age's new ideas... Tell him—

VALOMBRE, *interrupting*. I beg your pardon, monsieur! I have the greatest respect for my son's intelligence, but if he tries to teach me how to run my affairs...

LÉON. Father dear...

DE TENDALE, *to* VALOMBRE. Hardly, monsieur...

LÉON, *to* VALOMBRE. You know that we see eye to eye.

DE TENDALE, *to* LÉON. Monsieur de Valombre is wrong if he thinks I would make the son the preceptor to the father! Paternal authority is sacrosanct, after all. The first, and perhaps the only true authority in nature...

VALOMBRE. Yes... Well...

DE TENDALE, *continuing, to* VALOMBRE. My sole desire is to see the philosophy of youth come to terms with the experience of age. Please hear me out. I know you will understand.

VALOMBRE. Monsieur...

DE TENDALE. I was happy that my arrival fulfilled your hopes. As you know, it announces a long-awaited reform. Too long-awaited, my friend...

VALOMBRE. Yes, I...

DE TENDALE, *continuing*. But you surely cannot imagine... You are too intelligent and too humane to suppose that the Assemblée nationale would have dispatched me hither merely to effect a few paltry modifications in the governance of your colony and the merest fraction of its population.

VALOMBRE. But—

DE TENDALE. No, no... I come with the mission of remedying all abuse, all privilege, all oppression! The society, monsieur... Every class thereof is to partake in the rebirth! A rebirth which, to be just, must be universal!

VALOMBRE. But—

DE TENDALE. Ah, my friend... Does the sun mete out its rays in miserly fashion? Ought reason do so with its boons, monsieur?

VALOMBRE *and* LÉON *exchange bemused glances.*

CÉSAR JULIEN, *who has been listening with interest, to* DE TENDALE, *pointing to* VALOMBRE. Precisely what I have had the honor of suggesting... It is utterly unthinkable that only the big planters... Only the big plantation owners... That only the whites, monsieur, should have their slice of the pie! The classes that the law has ravished... *(To himself.)* Ravaged? *(Aloud.)* They have to be brought back into the society, monsieur! Undoubtably! Undoubtably!

DE TENDALE, *replying.* Quite so! You identify the heart of the matter, my friend. (CÉSAR JULIEN *beams with satisfaction.*) The difference between the races gives rise to an aristocracy of the most odious sort.

CÉSAR JULIEN. Exactly, monsieur... Take the whites and the mulattoes. They are all born equal. But your whites refuse to think of us as human beings, and they treat us like blacks!

DE TENDALE. Shameful, my friend! And an injustice that must be remedied, for one and all... The blacks as well as the mulattoes... I assure you, monsieur... Let a little time go by and all those scandalous inequalities will have disappeared into the past. Even the most revolting of all... Slavery itself...

VALOMBRE, ⎫   ⎡ Slavery...

LÉON,   ⎬ *together, shouting:* ⎨ What did he say?

CÉSAR JULIEN, ⎭   ⎣ Monsieur...

VALOMBRE, *to* DE TENDALE, *as* CÉSAR JULIEN *stands agape.* Monsieur...

LÉON, *to* DE TENDALE. Monsieur...

DE TENDALE, *misinterpreting their reaction.* Oh, I know what you must be thinking. A huge promise, to be sure... And devoutly to be wished... But we have already abolished so many abusive practices... Hope, my friends! Hope... And your hopes will be rewarded.

VALOMBRE, *trying to control his emotion.* My hopes, monsieur? Begging your pardon, but...

LÉON, *to* DE TENDALE. Monsieur...

VALOMBRE, *continuing.* My hopes, indeed! Abolish slavery? And what would you have us become? Would you have us beg our bread?

CÉSAR JULIEN, *to* DE TENDALE. Really, monsieur! Blacks are no more than chattel, pure and simple...

DE TENDALE. I say...

LÉON, *to* DE TENDALE. Please realize, monsieur... I respect your philosophy and the importance of your mission. But neither gives you the authority to speak so lightly about a time-honored institution. And one as fundamental as the right to own property, and the assurance of enjoying peace and tranquillity...

VALOMBRE, *under his breath.* Here, here!

DE TENDALE. But... My dear young friend... I fail to understand you. A power to reason as astute as yours—

LÉON. I know what I'm saying, monsieur. The Assemblée nationale has no right to humiliate us, to strip us of our possessions.

DE TENDALE. But human freedom cannot be compromised!

LÉON. Words, monsieur! Vague, high-sounding words! Before man thinks of freedom, he must think of justice!

DE TENDALE. You, young man...? Do I hear...? You, defending tyranny...?

LÉON. I'm defending my rights. Property is sacred. The Declaration of the Rights of Man, monsieur...

DE TENDALE. But...

LÉON, *continuing.* I reject all those subversive propositions that cast aside all difference. The difference between the black and the white, between heaven and earth... I fight against dreams of anarchy, monsieur...

VALOMBRE, *eager to quiet him.* Léon! Please—

DE TENDALE. No, no... Let him go on! Prejudice may annoy the philosopher, but it never enrages him. (*Turning to* MADAME DE VALOMBRE, *still seated with* CÉLESTINE, *addressing her almost jovially.*) You, dear lady... Perhaps you will come to my defense!

MADAME DE VALOMBRE. Me?

DE TENDALE. I appeal to your emotions... Your tender feelings, madame... Has the fate of the blacks not touched your heart a thousand times? Woman's sentiment has wrought such progress in our century.

MADAME DE VALOMBRE. Why yes, monsieur... I've often pitied the blacks, poor things...

DE TENDALE. Ah, I knew...

MADAME DE VALOMBRE. Working the way they do, out in the sun...
And without a hat...

CÉSAR JULIEN, *to* DE TENDALE. But monsieur, if I may say... Your
peasants in France are much more miserable than our slaves,
and they work a good deal harder.

DE TENDALE. The French farmer is free, monsieur. And freedom is
a possession that redeems all else!

VALOMBRE. Yes, but with no master to look after them... No one to
be concerned with their well-being, their health... With their
very life, monsieur! They are far more to be pitied!

DE TENDALE. Then why is it, my friend, that one never finds whites
willing to do the work of blacks?

VALOMBRE. Why, it's... it's because...

LÉON. Because of prejudice, monsieur! They fear they might be
taken for blacks... Confused with them...

DE TENDALE. Aha! Than you agree that distinction of caste based
on the color of one's skin is a prejudice, my friend.

LÉON. That's not what I said... But...

VALOMBRE, *to* DE TENDALE. These fine theories are beyond me,
monsieur. I only know that, without my slaves, the Assemblée
nationale may still have its coffee. It's the poor whites who
grow it. But they'll have to take it without sugar!

CÉLESTINE, *approaching* LÉON. You look concerned, brother dear.

LÉON. Bah! I can't help thinking, Célestine...

ROSINE *enters, down left.*

ROSINE, *to* MADAME DE VALOMBRE, *pointing across the footlights.* The *bon père,* madame...

MADAME DE VALOMBRE. Show him in, Rosine. (*To* VALOMBRE.) If I may...

VALOMBRE, *to* DE TENDALE. If monsieur has no objections...

    ROSINE *curtsies and exits, down left.*

DE TENDALE. None whatsoever! I shall see him with pleasure... Tell me, are your blacks superstitious?

VALOMBRE. They tend to be, monsieur. Somewhat... Especially the ones newly purchased in the trade, who are still rather simple. But the *bon père* is trying to rid them of superstition... Of foolish beliefs...

DE TENDALE, *misunderstanding.* Rid them of foolish beliefs? A priest? (*With a note of sarcasm.*) He must be a freethinker, this *bon père* of yours!

VALOMBRE, *on whom the irony is lost, misunderstanding in turn.* Perhaps... He is very eager to give them the sacraments, but we object, of course.[10]

DE TENDALE. Of course! You are too enlightened, I'm sure...

VALOMBRE. Indeed! No need to enlighten *them,* after all... With too much religion...

DE TENDALE, *aside.* Enlighten them? With religion? (*Aloud, to* VALOMBRE.) I fail to see...

LÉON, *noticing* THE CURÉ *approaching, down left, pointing.* There, monsieur... I'm sure he'll explain himself.

---

10. Abolitionists and Catholic priests in the colonies urged colonists to provide slaves with a Christian education and the opportunity to engage in religious practices.

DE TENDALE, *to himself.* A disciple of Rousseau, perhaps... Like his Vicaire Savoyard...[11]

THE CURÉ *enters, down left.*

THE CURÉ. Greetings, my honorable and distinguished friends. (*To* VALOMBRE.) Please pardon me, monsieur, if I fail to inquire at length of your health and that of your ladies.

VALOMBRE, *with a casual wave.* Please, *mon père...*

THE CURÉ. However, I bear some most disquieting information.

LÉON, *under his breath.* Another long-winded plea, no doubt!

VALOMBRE, *to* THE CURÉ. Oh?

LÉON, *under his breath.* Of all times!

THE CURÉ. Yes. A rider came by only moments ago... From the Saint-Louis-de-Morin parish, monsieur... And he brought word that the Morne-Noir plantation... The plantation of Monsieur Gernon de Patate Neuve, as you know...

VALOMBRE. Yes, yes...

THE CURÉ. He brought word that it was in flames.

CÉLESTINE *claps her hand to her mouth in shock.*

VALOMBRE. Good God!

MADAME DE VALOMBRE, *fanning herself.* Goodness me! Could they spread here?

---

11. Published in 1762, book IV of Rousseau's *Émile* contains the famous "Profession de foi du vicaire savoyard," which provides a model for introducing young people to religion.

THE CURÉ, *continuing.* But the most upsetting news is that it was the blacks themselves who set the fire. That it is an insurrection, my friends, in no uncertain terms...

LÉON. Insurrection? A rebellion, you mean!

THE CURÉ. No... "Insurrection," I think...

DE TENDALE *and* VALOMBRE, *together, to each other.* You see?

THE CURÉ, *continuing.* I believe that is the word that was used in France.

VALOMBRE, *to* DE TENDALE. Free the blacks now, indeed!

DE TENDALE, *giving him tit for tat.* Dare to keep them enslaved!

THE CURÉ. But I fear there is more. It appears that in the insurrection... Or in the rebellion... Or simply in the fire... It appears that Monsieur Gernon has perished.

CÉLESTINE. Good heavens!

THE CURÉ. Some say he was merely burned to death, but others say it was the blacks...

VALOMBRE. God help us!

CÉSAR JULIEN. The blacks!

MADAME DE VALOMBRE. Goodness me!

CÉSAR JULIEN. Yes! It must have been the blacks!

DE TENDALE, *shaking his head.* It was bound to happen.

CÉSAR JULIEN. Who can doubt it?

THE CURÉ. As you can well imagine, my heart is most troubled. How can one hope to intercede in their favor now? True, Monsieur Gernon was rich, and the harshest master for miles around...

VALOMBRE. Poor Gernon...

THE CURÉ. But he was no less their master.

VALOMBRE. I can't believe...

LÉON, *to* DE TENDALE. So! Loose the Beast, my friend!

DE TENDALE. Please! You must remain calm! You must see this as a
warning, a foreboding... An insurrection is proof that freedom
cannot be postponed. True, we must deplore the misfortunes,
and shed a tear for the victims. (*To* THE CURÉ.) But, as you say,
they were wicked masters. Their tyranny has brought destruction down upon their heads. *(To the others.)* Let that be your
consolation... Was their blood so pure, I ask you?

VALOMBRE. At a time like this, monsieur, discussion is pointless. Good
people must stand together! Yes, we must see this as a warning...
A warning to every plantation owner to redouble his vigilance...

DE TENDALE. Monsieur...

VALOMBRE. My blacks are about to enjoy a pause in their labors.
Please join in helping maintain their spirit of service. A careless
word could have dire consequences, monsieur.

DE TENDALE. Quite so, my friend! Rest assured, I shall support
you in every way I can. Heaven forbid that I provoke the least
violence whatever. "Light must shine over the mind as daylight
shines over delicate eyes." *(To* LÉON, *who ignores him.)* Voltaire,
I think...

CÉSAR JULIEN. These blacks are clever! There's no putting anything
past them... They're not just stupid animals!

DE TENDALE. But monsieur, I thought I heard you say...

THE CURÉ. Alas! If only they had been permitted to come to
church... If only one might have taught them the Gospel... We

would have been spared this calamitous misfortune. But the ways of the Lord are impossible to comprehend!

> MORIN *and* GALAOR *enter, down left, followed by* HÉLÈNE, CLOTILDE, VÉNUS, *and* HERMIONE, *carrying fruits and flowers on banana leaves. Other male and female blacks enter as well, among them* JEAN-PIERRE, JUAN, ALMANZOR, *and* TÉLÉMAQUE. *Several slaves are carrying in a long table and chairs, which they place down center.*

MORIN, *to* DE TENDALE. Monsieur, my blacks insist on thanking monsieur in person for this pause in their labors.

DE TENDALE. And I accept their thanks with delight!

> MORIN *withdraws right, to the shed, and stands watching the proceedings with obvious dissatisfaction.*

VALOMBRE, *to* MADAME DE VALOMBRE. My love... While our blacks are amusing themselves, perhaps monsieur would enjoy watching them at their sport... *(Pointing upstage.)* From the shade of the trees...

MADAME DE VALOMBRE. Of course, *chéri.*

> *She summons several blacks, motions to them to move the table up center. As they do so,* HÉLÈNE, CLOTILDE, VÉNUS, *and* HERMIONE *present their offering to* DE TENDALE.

DE TENDALE, *nodding to them.* Thank you, my dears. *(To the blacks who have moved the table.)* And you, my friends...

GALAOR. Monsieur can see how much they appreciate his kindness and how happy they are.

He stands center, eating a piece of fruit, preparing to watch the revels.

DE TENDALE. I hope they will appreciate even more one day. (*To* VALOMBRE.) You see, monsieur. If one knows how to treat them... They seem so well-behaved, and not at all unhappy...

While they continue to converse, JEAN-JACQUES *enters, down left, and sets the table. In the meantime,* LÉON *has joined* CÉLESTINE, *up left.*

CÉLESTINE. Please, brother dear... Tell me...

LÉON. The Morne-Noir plantation, Célestine...

CÉLESTINE. Frightful, isn't it!

LÉON. Worse than frightful! Now what?

JEAN-JACQUES. Supper is served, madame.

MADAME DE VALOMBRE, *to* VALOMBRE. My dear...

She stands up and approaches the table.

VALOMBRE. Come, my friends... (*To* THE CURÉ.) Please join us, *mon père*... Next to madame... Célestine, next to Monsieur de Tendale... César, here... And Léon? (*Calling to him.*) Léon...

LÉON, *preoccupied.* Yes, papá...

He sits down beside VALOMBRE *as the others take their places.*

VALOMBRE, *watching the blacks, who are forming groups, beginning to dance, clap hands, chant, etc.* Free as birds!... Happy as princes!

DE TENDALE. Yes... *(Under his breath.)* For the moment... Then what, I wonder...

VALOMBRE, *serving the others.* A lobster bisque, my friends...

CÉSAR JULIEN. Splendid!

DE TENDALE. Much obliged...

VALOMBRE, *to himself.* None for me... *(Aside, to* LÉON.*)* I have no appetite, I'm afraid... Poor Gernon...

> *As the blacks celebrate and the supper proceeds,* JEAN-PIERRE, JUAN, ALMANZOR, *and* TÉLÉMAQUE *have moved to the stage-right end of the table and stand conversing in hushed tones.*

JUAN, *pointing to* DE TENDALE. Is he the one?

JEAN-PIERRE. Yes.

JUAN. How does Timur know him?

JEAN-PIERRE. He doesn't.

JUAN. But he told us—

JEAN-PIERRE. He told us to be careful and... Keep quiet!... Ah! How I wish tonight would come!

ALMANZOR. And you're sure we'll have guns?

JEAN-PIERRE. What's wrong, coward! Don't we have teeth and nails? Fangs and claws?

TÉLÉMAQUE *to* ALMANZOR, *gazing at the food.* Look at all that food, amigo!

ALMANZOR. Shouldn't we talk to him, Jean-Pierre?

TÉLÉMAQUE. Damn hungry, those whites!

JEAN-PIERRE, *replying to* ALMANZOR. Certainly not!

CLOTILDE *approaches the group.*

CLOTILDE, *to* JUAN. Come dance the bamboula, Juan.[12] You and me...

JEAN-PIERRE, *overhearing, to* JUAN. I wouldn't. (*Pointing to* HÉLÈNE.) Not if that one is dancing too!

JUAN. Who cares?

HERMIONE, *to* JEAN-PIERRE. You're right, Jean-Pierre. But we're kicking her out!

JEAN-PIERRE, *to* JUAN, *whispering.* Besides, you've got other things to do!

HERMIONE, *to* ALMANZOR. Come, Zozor!

HERMIONE, CLOTILDE, ALMANZOR, *and* TÉLÉMAQUE *go off to join the dance, as* JUAN *slips off, inconspicuously, up left.* JEAN-PIERRE *remains up right, watching.* HÉLÈNE, *brooding, remains with* VÉNUS, *down left.*

VÉNUS, *to* HÉLÈNE. What's the trouble, child? Why such a sad face? Is it those nasty things Hermione keeps saying?

HÉLÈNE, *softly.* No...

VÉNUS. You know, the young master is really very nice. There's no reason to eat your heart out just because he wants to—

HÉLÈNE. Thank you, Vénus, but you don't understand.

VÉNUS. Well then, brood all you like. Just don't go kill yourself with voodoo spells, love.

12. The bamboula is a dance performed to the beat of Haitian drums.

HÉLÈNE. If only I could... But no... He would still think... He would still believe...

VÉNUS. He?

HÉLÈNE. Timur!... He would still think... No, I have to live. For him, Vénus! For my Touko! My Touko!

The supper continues. As the blacks dance and chant, VALOMBRE *tosses fruits and sweets to them.*

VALOMBRE, *to* DE TENDALE, *explaining.* Guava, monsieur... And kumquats... (*To* MADAME DE VALOMBRE.) We needn't take our fruit at table, my love. Monsieur doesn't stand on ceremony.

DE TENDALE. Please, consider me a friend...

LÉON, *standing up, to* VALOMBRE. May I be excused, papá?

VALOMBRE. Of course, son... (*To* DE TENDALE, *holding up the fruit.*) Delicious, aren't they!

MADAME DE VALOMBRE. Célestine, be a dear and serve the coffee.

LÉON, *up left, pacing back and forth, to himself, watching the blacks.* Look at them! Dancing... Singing...

CÉLESTINE, *to* MADAME DE VALOMBRE. Yes, mammá.

LÉON, *to himself.* They seem so happy, so peaceful... I wonder... (*As* CÉLESTINE *serves the coffee, then sits down next to her mother and* THE CURÉ.) What can it all be hiding? (*Casually approaching* HÉLÈNE *as the others sip their coffee.*) Ah! Hélène... Dear child... (*To* VÉNUS, *as* HÉLÈNE *turns her head aside.*) And you, you old—

VÉNUS, *interrupting.* Monsieur!

LÉON. Not dancing, I see? *(To* HÉLÈNE, *who is still not looking at him.)* Nor you...

VÉNUS, *to herself.* He spoke to me!

LÉON, *to* HÉLÈNE, *continuing.* Why aren't you dancing either?

VÉNUS, *to herself.* A first time for everything!

HÉLÈNE, *looking him in the eye, contemptuously.* Why?

LÉON, *under his breath.* Curious child! *(He moves off, right, watching the dancing, and musing.)* Something... I don't know what...

VALOMBRE, *to* DE TENDALE. How do you find our coffee, monsieur?

LÉON, *to himself, still musing.* But something is in the air...

DE TENDALE, *to* VALOMBRE, *replying.* Superb, my friend. A mocha, if I am not mistaken... The aristocrat of the bean!

VALOMBRE. Indeed! Only transplanted to our soil... I'll wager you agree that we have many a marvel here in the colonies!

CÉSAR JULIEN, *who has been unsuccessfully trying now and then to break into the conversation, to* DE TENDALE, *holding up a bottle.* A glass of rum, monsieur?

Without waiting for a reply, he pours him a glass.

DE TENDALE, *sipping.* Ah! Exquisite beverage!... What a shame that the memories of bondage must infuse so many a pleasure!

VALOMBRE, *as* DE TENDALE *empties the glass.* Monsieur...

DE TENDALE, *holding it up.* This one costs the price of the African's toil and sweat.

CÉSAR JULIEN, *assuming that* DE TENDALE *is gesturing for more, refills the glass.*

DE TENDALE. I say...

VALOMBRE. The Jamaicans can say what they please, monsieur. There is no finer rum in all the islands.

DE TENDALE, *to* MADAME DE VALOMBRE. Madame, if I may ask... These well-dressed blacks who serve you... Are they slaves as well?

MADAME DE VALOMBRE. Yes, they are domestics.

DE TENDALE, *nodding.* Aha... And obviously you treat them according to that touching definition. To wit. "Domestics are merely friends in unfortunate circumstances."

MADAME DE VALOMBRE. Friends? Heavens! They cost us enough, I assure you!

CÉSAR JULIEN, *to* DE TENDALE, *pointing to the blacks.* A charming scene, monsieur, don't you agree?

MADAME DE VALOMBRE, *continuing, pointing to one of the blacks.* Why, that one alone cost my husband three hundred *pistoles*![13]

CÉSAR JULIEN, *continuing.* Typical rustic revels...

DE TENDALE, *to* VALOMBRE. Monsieur, with your permission, might we join these fine folk? I am eager to know their feelings.

VALOMBRE. As you wish, monsieur. Only please... Be discreet.

DE TENDALE. Certainly, my friend... (*To* LÉON.) Will you join us?

LÉON, *nodding.* Monsieur...

13. *Pistole* is the French name given to a Spanish gold coin.

MADAME DE VALOMBRE, CÉLESTINE, and THE CURÉ *remain seated as* DE TENDALE, VALOMBRE, CÉSAR JULIEN, *and* LÉON *stroll among the blacks.* THE CURÉ *begins dozing.*

DE TENDALE. I am certain that, if we engage them in conversation, we shall find them possessed of reason and a moral sense. Nature, everywhere, is quite the same... *(To* GALAOR, *center, chewing on his fruit.)* You seem to be enjoying that fruit, young man...

GALAOR. Oh yes, monsieur Frenchman...

DE TENDALE. Are there such delicious fruits in Africa?

GALAOR. I... I don't know.

DE TENDALE. What?

LÉON. He's a Creole, monsieur. Born here, in the colonies...

DE TENDALE, *surprised.* Oh? I thought there were no Creole blacks left. I thought that all the newborns were done away with or left to perish...

LÉON. A vicious rumor, monsieur!

CÉSAR JULIEN. A total exaggeration!

LÉON. One of many spread against us...

CÉSAR JULIEN. At least one third of them survive... Yes... A good third, I think.

DE TENDALE, *to* GALAOR. Tell me, young man. Are you content here? Have you ever thought of changing your situation?

VALOMBRE, *taken aback.* Monsieur de Tendale!

GALAOR. Me? Work for a different master?... Oh no! I hope not...

DE TENDALE. No, my friend. Not a different master... A different kind of life...

VALOMBRE, *uneasy.* Monsieur...

GALAOR. Oh no, monsieur Frenchman... Things can be hard here sometimes. Some of the people... But we all get along.

DE TENDALE. Aha... *(To himself.)* Such calm acceptance... Such patience... *(To* VALOMBRE *and* LÉON.) I confess, I would have expected them to display more bitterness toward their enslavement, my friends. Such gentle creatures...

LÉON. Best not question them too much, monsieur.

DE TENDALE. Would you not have me see with my own eyes... *(Noticing* JEAN-PIERRE, *still standing upright.)* Ah! Perhaps that strapping young devil... *(To* JEAN-PIERRE.) Good day, my friend.

JEAN-PIERRE. Good day, white man.

DE TENDALE, *to* VALOMBRE. Is he from Africa?

VALOMBRE. Yes, monsieur.

DE TENDALE, *to* JEAN-PIERRE. How far you are from your country, young man! You must miss it...

VALOMBRE, *to* DE TENDALE. Please, monsieur...

DE TENDALE, *continuing.* With your deserts, your forests...

VALOMBRE. Please...

DE TENDALE, *continuing.* But surely you have copious pleasures here as well. The joys of civilization... Nature's creature becomes society's child, as it were. *(To* LÉON *and* VALOMBRE, *as* JEAN-PIERRE *gives a little nod.)* You see? He quite understands. *(To* JEAN-PIERRE.) Well now! Be strong! One day you will be perfectly happy... Happy and free...

VALOMBRE, *in an anxious whisper.* I beg your pardon...

DE TENDALE. One has to give them hope...

VALOMBRE. Yes, but...

JEAN-PIERRE, *under his breath.* He seems to know it's for tonight!

LÉON, *to* DE TENDALE. Really, monsieur...

DE TENDALE, *changing the subject, to* VALOMBRE. And the women? What are they like?... I confess, I find them singularly unappealing. Repulsive, even... Far be it from me to try to understand the taste that our colonists have for black women... (LÉON *winces.*) But tyranny enjoys corrupting its victims. One truly must be depraved to be moved by such passions. Ah, the abuse of power, my friends...

LÉON. But...

DE TENDALE. Vice pushed to utterly genteel extremes...

CÉSAR JULIEN, *to* DE TENDALE. As they say, monsieur, "chacun à son goût." And we try not to question color, considering...

He beams proudly.

VALOMBRE, *to* DE TENDALE, *in a whisper.* Again... I must ask you—

DE TENDALE. Ah! Pardon me... I forgot myself, I'm afraid. The emotion, you know... *(Pointing to* HÉLÈNE, *down left.)* That one, for example... Young as she is, who could ever be moved to love such a face?

LÉON. Oh? Aren't they wretched enough, monsieur, without your insults? Why take from them all that they have left? The gift of being loved...

DE TENDALE. Oh?

LÉON. The heart cares nothing for the whims of our eyes and all our meaningless distinctions!

DE TENDALE, *clapping*. Bravo, my young friend! You are being converted after all, I see! Felicitations! (*Approaching* HÉLÈNE.) What is your name, my dear?

HÉLÈNE. People here call me Hélène.

DE TENDALE. And does our Hélène have a lover?

HÉLÈNE. I... I have a husband...

DE TENDALE. And have you any children?

HÉLÈNE. One, monsieur... But he has gone to Guinea.

DE TENDALE. Oh? He has returned?

VALOMBRE. She means that he is dead, monsieur.

DE TENDALE. Ah... (*To* HÉLÈNE.) And your husband, my dear? Where is he now?

HÉLÈNE. I don't know, white friend. *(Sadly.)* I swear, I don't know...

VALOMBRE, *to* LÉON. What's troubling her, son?

HÉLÈNE, *continuing*. He didn't tell me...

VALOMBRE, *continuing*. And who is this husband of hers?

LÉON. I... I wouldn't know!

HERMIONE, *overhearing, to* VALOMBRE. Her husband is the carpenter, and he's in the forest. He left because of her.

VALOMBRE, *to* HERMIONE. The runaway, you mean?

CÉSAR JULIEN, *to* HERMIONE. Because of her, you say?

HERMIONE. Yes. Because she was unfaithful...

HÉLÈNE. She's lying! That's not true!

LÉON, *to* HERMIONE. You! Be quiet!

HÉLÈNE, *to* LÉON. No, no... You... Let her speak!

VALOMBRE, *to* DE TENDALE. Household affairs, Monsieur de Tendale...
Best we stay out of them, I daresay...

DE TENDALE, *to* VALOMBRE *and* LÉON. But feelings, my friends!...
Emotions!... The noble cry of nature...

> *During the preceding,* JUAN *enters cautiously, up left, and
> approaches* JEAN-PIERRE.

JUAN, *whispering to him.* People, Jean-Pierre... At the coconut trees...

JEAN-PIERRE, *whispering.* Ah! Timur... I'm on my way. *(Pointing to
the blacks.)* Have the rest of them join me. But not all at once...

> *He exits, up left.*

DE TENDALE, *to the blacks.* My dear friends... *(They stop dancing as
he begins to speak.)* My fascinating and unfortunate children...
I am happy with what I see. I had hoped that oppression would
not have corrupted your hearts...

VALOMBRE, *whispering.* Monsieur...

DE TENDALE, *continuing.* That it would not have dimmed your reason... And I find that you are still human beings, with all the
human dignity that nature intended. Yes, I realize that you deserve all the rights that such a gift entails.

VALOMBRE, *whispering.* Please! What are you—

DE TENDALE, *ignoring him.* But no need to fear. In time, my
friends... I ask only that you understand that, after centuries

of abuse, reform must come slowly. Slowly and carefully, with thought and consideration... (VALOMBRE *heaves a sigh.*) And so I hope and trust that you will remain patient, and prudent, and devoted to your masters...

VALOMBRE, *to himself.* Good... Good...

DE TENDALE, *continuing.* And that you will realize that respect for order is the very foundation of freedom!

> As VALOMBRE *applauds discreetly,* ALMANZOR, JUAN, *and the other blacks raise an echoing cry of "Freedom! Freedom!" casting meaningful glances at one another, and waking* THE CURÉ *with a start.*

VALOMBRE, *to* DE TENDALE. Monsieur! Heaven help us!

LÉON, *to* VALOMBRE. They make me shudder... (*Pointing to* DE TEN-DALE.) And so does he!

DE TENDALE, *still addressing the blacks.* So I ask you to wait with confidence for the day... That day that will doubtless dawn in the heavens above you... That day when, bending gently to philosophy's will, the government of France will bestow upon you the boons long claimed for your race by the likes of Montesquieu and the Abbé Raynal...[14]

VALOMBRE, *under his breath.* Never!

DE TENDALE. When there will be no need for you to follow the scurrilous example of your brothers on the Morne-Noir plantation...

14. Charles de Secondat, baron de Montesquieu, and Guillaume Raynal were the foremost eighteenth-century French antislavery writers. Although Montesquieu viewed slavery as against natural law, he acknowledged its appropriateness in certain countries. Raynal predicted that a black leader would emerge; Toussaint Louverture is often seen as the fulfillment of that prediction.

*The blacks mutter amongst themselves, with questions like
"What does he mean?" "What did they do?" etc.*

LÉON, *under his breath.* Good God!

DE TENDALE, *continuing.* Your brothers who—would you believe
it, my dear friends?—

VALOMBRE, *in a whisper.* No, no... Please...

DE TENDALE. Who burned the plantation to the ground, and slit
their master's throat!

ALMANZOR, *shouting.* Burned the plantation!

> *The blacks, excited, echo his shout: "Burned the planta-
> tion! Burned the plantation!"*

JUAN, *shouting.* And slit their master's throat!

> *The blacks, growing more and more excited, echo: "Their
> master's throat..." "Slit their master's throat..."*

VALOMBRE. Léon...

LÉON, *noticeably shaken.* It's too much, papá!

DE TENDALE, *misjudging the blacks' reaction, addressing them.* Ah yes!
I see that you recoil in horror. I knew you would. I knew that your
hearts could not fail to be moved!... Hold fast, worthy Africans!
Hold fast to your noble sentiments! Entrust yourselves with
confidence to the protective vision of the Assemblée nationale!
Prove yourselves deserving of the blessing it readies for you!
Your submission to our laws, your wisdom, your human virtues...
These alone will hasten the moment of your deliverance! The
happy moment when, at last, you shall be free!

The blacks, jumping for joy, raise a cacophony of cries:
"Free, free!" "We will be free!" "At last, at last!" etc.

LÉON, *to* DE TENDALE. You thoughtless... What are you doing?

DE TENDALE, *ignoring him.* How touching!

VALOMBRE, *to* DE TENDALE. You're making my blood run cold, monsieur!

CÉSAR JULIEN, *to* DE TENDALE. Monsieur, I fear... I...

DE TENDALE, *ignoring them, continuing.* These poor, dear folk...

CÉSAR JULIEN, *continuing.* I fear you have been a trifle indiscreet...

JUAN, *to one of the blacks, in a whisper.* Come. It's time.

He and the black exit, up left.

VALOMBRE, *summoning* MORIN, *who has been standing right, observing the preceding.* Speak to them, Morin! Say something...

MORIN, *to the blacks still left.* Listen to me, you! You hear what the good white man is saying... Obedience, you understand? Obedience and work! And not a word, you hear? The first one who has something to say gets twenty lashes. The second will be put in irons. And the third will be seized and brought to justice!

VALOMBRE, *with a sigh of relief.* Ah...

MORIN. You understand? *(As the blacks grumble their surprise and displeasure.)* Now dance! *(Under his breath.)* Damn you! *(Aloud.)* Dance!

VALOMBRE, DE TENDALE, THE CURÉ, *and* CÉSAR JULIEN *come downstage, followed by* MADAME DE VALOMBRE, *still fanning herself.* LÉON *and* CÉLESTINE *hang back for a moment.*

DE TENDALE, *to* VALOMBRE. I think my words have produced the desired effect.

LÉON, *under his breath.* Like a torch and a dagger!

VALOMBRE. Come... Monsieur has done enough for one day...

MADAME DE VALOMBRE, *to the men.* You must be tired after your long walk. Wouldn't you like to rest in the salon?

DE TENDALE, *as they exit along the path, down left.* When one is an apostle of humanity, madame, one knows no fatigue.

VALOMBRE, DE TENDALE, CÉSAR JULIEN, *and* MADAME DE VALOMBRE *exit.* THE CURÉ *follows them out, shaking his head.*

CÉLESTINE, *to* LÉON. Oh, Léon! What a frightful situation! How upset you look!

LÉON. Upset? I'm beside myself, Célestine! Good God in heaven!

CÉLESTINE. Please, brother dear...

LÉON. So many emotions... I hardly know where I am!

CÉLESTINE. Try to control yourself. For me... See how I tremble? Why? Who can say?... I need you to be calm. I need your courage...

LÉON. Oh? Courage, I have my fill! If only I knew what to think... If only...

They exit along the path, down left.

MORIN, *angrily, to the remaining blacks.* Good! That's enough dancing for today! The sun is going down... *(Motioning them off.)* Go!... Get out!... You're making too much noise!... Out! Out!

As he chases them off, up left, HERMIONE *passes in front of* HÉLÈNE, *still down left.*

HERMIONE. Of all the nerve!... To tell them all that she and Timur... Oh! Of all the... When everybody knows that she and the young master...

She exits in a huff, up left.

MORIN, *approaching* HÉLÈNE, *to himself.* Aha! Our little Hélène isn't joining the others? I understand... *(Sarcastically.)* She mustn't stray too far from his house, after all! *(Aloud, to* HÉLÈNE, *patronizingly.)* Good evening, my dear... Not leaving, I see... As you like... As you like... I trust you find what you're waiting for...

He gives a sarcastic little laugh and exits, down left.

HÉLÈNE, *alone.* Too much... It's too much... I haven't the strength to put up with their taunts. They all believe what my Touko believes. How can I prove them wrong? If only he were here, I would make him believe me. *(Sighing.)* Oh! What would I say? At least he would pity me. At least, not hate me... No, he is too kind, too good. Am I to blame if my arms are too weak? Too weak to defend me?... I called out to him... Called his name in my voice choked with sorrow... Called out to my friend, my only friend... My African friend!... If only he had heard me, he would have come to save me. He would have avenged me... Who knows? Perhaps he would have taken me off... Off to join his flight... Ah! To be with him, together, in the forests! Just as we were at home, when we were young! Instead of alone, each one of us now... Him, in his peril, and me, in my despair! If they catch him he will die... Die, cursing my name... And I will die too, with no pardon, no farewell... Oh mother! Mother dear... What would you say if you saw her now, your poor Badia, all alone... Abandoned by her Touko... Alone, without your bosom to comfort her, his arm to protect her... Ah! Too much... It's too much... But *Bon Dié bon*...[15] *(With a desperate sigh.)* Now nothing for Badia, poor Badia, but to die... Oh, Touko!... Poor Touko!

> *She crouches, left, at the foot of a catalpa tree, partially hidden. As she sits weeping silently in the waning light,* JEAN-PIERRE *and* JUAN *enter, up left, crossing quickly right.*

JEAN-PIERRE, *angrily.* Oh! The cowards! The traitors!... What else could we expect from such rabble! Such scum!

JUAN, *looking about, not noticing* HÉLÈNE. We can talk. No one is here.

JEAN-PIERRE. Excuses... Excuses... We give them three rifles. But no, they want more... They don't want to hang behind, so we put them in the lead...

HÉLÈNE, *looking up from her sobbing, aside.* Oh! Two blacks...

JEAN-PIERRE. Then they say they want to wait... Too many people in the house... And Sunday the codfish is being given out! Did you ever—

HÉLÈNE, *peering at them through the shadows, to herself.* Who, I wonder...

JUAN. What the devil did you expect?

JEAN-PIERRE. All kinds of stupid, idiotic excuses!

JUAN. It's their first time, Jean-Pierre! If they knew what rebellions are like... If they had seen one before...

HÉLÈNE, *aside.* Ah! Jean-Pierre...

15. *Bon Dié bon* is a common Creole expression meaning "God is good."

JEAN-PIERRE. And the ones at Morne-Noir? It wasn't their first?

JUAN. The *bon père* said—

JEAN-PIERRE. Timur told me all about it. Everything, burned down... Everything, except the rum and the whiskey!

HÉLÈNE, *overhearing, aside.* Timur?

JEAN-PIERRE, *continuing.* And the master, hacked to bits!... What a lovely sight it must have been!

JUAN. Yes, the time was ripe...

JEAN-PIERRE. Damn it, Juan! Poor Timur is beside himself. He was counting on tonight.

> HÉLÈNE *pricks up her ears.*

JUAN. Of course! He has no time to lose... Is he gone?

JEAN-PIERRE. No! He refuses to leave!

HÉLÈNE, *aside.* What?

JEAN-PIERRE. He thinks there's still hope...

HÉLÈNE, *aside.* Timur? Here?... *(Loud enough to be overheard.)* I must see him!

> She stands up and begins to move off, up left.

JUAN. Who's that? Someone listening...

JEAN-PIERRE, *noticing her.* It's that snake in the grass! (*To* HÉLÈNE.) Stop, you! You're not leaving!

> He seizes her.

HÉLÈNE, *struggling.* Oh! Let me go! Let me go!... I want to see him! I must!

JEAN-PIERRE. Oh yes! So you can betray him again?... No, no! Once is enough, you... you viper!

JUAN. Careful! She'll go tell her white lover everything!

HÉLÈNE. My... But he's not! He's not...

> *As she continues to struggle and protest,* JUAN *notices* LÉON *about to appear along the path, down left.*

JUAN, *pointing.* Look! There he is!

HÉLÈNE. But...

JEAN-PIERRE. You see? She's waiting for him, the slut!

HÉLÈNE. No, I—

JEAN-PIERRE. If only I could choke her without a sound! If only... (*Releasing her and pushing her away, to* JUAN.) Come! We can still warn Timur and give him time to escape. (*To* HÉLÈNE.) And you! If you follow us, I'll strangle you on the spot! You hear me?

> *He and* JUAN *exit quickly, up left. As* HÉLÈNE, *trembling, hides behind the catalpa tree,* LÉON *enters without seeing her.*

LÉON, *upstage, obviously disturbed.* Good God! What can I do? Which way should I turn? So many emotions, so many thoughts... That Frenchman who tries my patience, that woman who breaks my heart!... Racked by doubts... Bitten by remorse... Can it be that all my principles were nothing but smoke? Perilous dreams... Or can it be that my father and I are tyrants?... No! No! How could that be? So many have done the same! For all these years!

(Pausing to reflect.) But have they?... The same?... Have they done what I have done?... That woman... She and I... Oh! That look of hers... The humiliation... The scorn, the pride... They chill me to the bone at the slightest thought! And that face, forever before my eyes... And... *(Suddenly noticing* HÉLÈNE.*)* God! There... Hélène, it's you... *(As she turns to leave.)* No, please! Don't go... Don't... I beg you—

He approaches her.

HÉLÈNE. Stay away, you beast! Stay—

LÉON. Hélène...

HÉLÈNE. Stay away!

LÉON. Hélène... There's no need to be afraid! Please... Don't look at me like that!

HÉLÈNE. You... You...

LÉON. What's wrong? What did I do?

HÉLÈNE. What did you do? What... *(Recoiling as he approaches.)* No, no! Stay away!

LÉON. Please! Don't be afraid! It's no longer a master standing before you... Threatening you... A master, drunk with power and lusting with desire!... No... Never would I harm you! Never would I dare!... *(Stammering.)* It's... I... It's a lover, Hélène!

HÉLÈNE, *fending him off.* Poisonous words, monsieur! Vicious traps!

LÉON. Yes, a lover... A lover who finds you more beautiful even than when he held you in his arms!

HÉLÈNE. Please...

LÉON. You're frightened... I understand... Only, tell me you don't hate me!

HÉLÈNE. I do! I do!

LÉON. Oh! Spare me...

HÉLÈNE, *furiously.* I detest you!

LÉON. No! No!... I beg you! Spare me those looks that stun me with grief... That mortify my pride... If you knew how I suffer... If you knew how humbled, how crushed I feel... Please! Don't say you hate me! I mean you no harm. I... Yes, I... I'll say it... I'll say those words that fill me with shame... Words I try to resist, but I cannot... I cannot... Oh, Hélène, I... I love you!

TIMUR *appears suddenly atop the hill, upstage.*

TIMUR, *aside.* Oh! Jean-Pierre was right! There they are! Together...

HÉLÈNE, *to* LÉON. You love me?

TIMUR, *pounding his chest, angrily, aside.* Oh, my heart!

HÉLÈNE, *to* LÉON. You love me, you say?

LÉON, *pleading.* Hélène...

HÉLÈNE. Well, listen to me! You disgust me, you dog!

TIMUR, *aside.* What?

HÉLÈNE. I loathe you!

TIMUR, *sighing.* Ah...

LÉON. No! Don't say that! God in heaven! Why can't I find the words?

TIMUR, *aside.* She said... She...

LÉON, *continuing.* Why won't you understand? Yes! I love you! I love you! You... So beautiful, so... My heart is yours... My head... My pride, Hélène... My life itself... I... I don't know what I feel. If you have any pity... Oh! Pardon me, Hélène! I'm begging you! Begging...

He falls to his knees.

TIMUR, *aside.* On his knees? The white devil...

HÉLÈNE, *to* LÉON. Pardon you, you beast!... Why? Why should I believe that same sweet tone, that same gentle look, as when you came to toy with me? When you gave me that foul brew to dull my senses, and...

TIMUR, *aside, enraged.* Oh!

HÉLÈNE, *continuing.* ...and when you took me... Who knows how?... Dragged me to the banana trees...

TIMUR, *aside.* The swine!

HÉLÈNE. ...struggling, weeping, screaming... And you tied my hands... And you... you... Oh, Touko! Forgive me...

She collapses on the ground.

TIMUR, *leaping down from the hill, with a terrifying shout, to* LÉON. You're a dead man, you—

LÉON. What?... Good God! *(Shouting.)* Help! Help!...

He seizes the shotgun, left against the tree by CÉSAR JULIEN, *and shoots at* TIMUR, *who falls to the ground.*

HÉLÈNE, *jumping, running to* TIMUR, *bending over him.* Touko! My Touko!

LÉON. Oh!

As HÉLÈNE *remains crouched, everyone comes running down left, from the house. Blacks, entering up left, fill the stage.*

VALOMBRE. A shot!...

MADAME DE VALOMBRE, *fanning herself.* Léon!

VALOMBRE. It was a shot!

CÉLESTINE, *to* LÉON. Brother dear!

MADAME DE VALOMBRE, *to* LÉON. Are you hurt?

LÉON. Please, mammá! It's nothing.

DE TENDALE, *noticing* TIMUR *on the ground.* Look! A poor black!... He's bleeding...

The blacks milling about, upstage, looking on, mutter and groan appropriately: "Oh, who...," "What happened?" "Who is it?" etc.

HÉLÈNE, *to* TIMUR, *cradling his head.* Ah! You're alive! My Touko, you're alive!

VALOMBRE. But who...

TIMUR, *weakly, to* HÉLÈNE. Badia... My Badia...

He kisses her.

VALOMBRE, *to* LÉON. Please, son, tell me...

LÉON. That wretch... He tried to kill me...

MADAME DE VALOMBRE. Oh!

CÉLESTINE. Léon... Brother dear...

> As HÉLÈNE, *disconsolate, stands aside,* MORIN *bends over* TIMUR.

MORIN, *to* VALOMBRE. It's the carpenter, monsieur. The runaway...

> *The blacks mutter in surprise: "It's Timur!" "Look, it's him!" etc.*

MADAME DE VALOMBRE, *trying not to faint.* Good heavens!

MORIN. Well, we've got him now! He won't escape again!

MADAME DE VALOMBRE, *tugging at her bodice.* Somebody, unlace me... Oh!...

MORIN, *looking* TIMUR *over.* Only a broken arm...

MADAME DE VALOMBRE. Before I swoon...

TIMUR, *to himself, weakly.* And my revenge?

VALOMBRE. Put him in irons! Take him away!

TIMUR, *to himself.* Later... Later...

DE TENDALE, *shaking his head.* Tsk tsk tsk! What a lesson for us all!... When we forget the Rights of Man... The Rights of Man...

End of Act III

ACT IV

The ground-floor salon. Up center, a fireplace. Up right, the door to Madame de Valombre's room. Down left, a door leading to the other rooms. Center, a loveseat. Up right and down left, an armchair. Down right, a table and chair, facing forward, with writing implements. Other appropriate furnishings.

At rise, Monsieur de Valombre is seated at the table, writing. Monsieur de Tendale, dressed to leave, is pacing back and forth. Léon and Célestine are seated on the loveseat next to one another. Madame de Valombre is standing in front of them. The Curé is in the armchair, up right, dozing from time to time.

LÉON, *to* CÉLESTINE. I'm so sorry that I gave you such concern, sister dear.

CÉLESTINE, *smiling.* Tsk tsk tsk! Poor thing... Then beg me to forgive you!

LÉON. You still love your brother?

CÉLESTINE. Do you have to ask, Léon?

LÉON. Ah, Célestine... Simple affection is so much a part of living that in time we even forget that we have it... Like breathing... But stop breathing, or stop being loved, and we die.

CÉLESTINE. Goodness! How pleasant...

MADAME DE VALOMBRE. Children dear... *(She kisses them in turn.)* I'm afraid today has taken a frightful toll on my nerves. *(Taking* CÉLESTINE'S *hands in hers.)* Célestine, love... You must be tired. You feel warm... A trifle feverish, perhaps?

CÉLESTINE. Oh no, mammá.

MADAME DE VALOMBRE. Best we all retire. *(Nodding toward* DE TENDALE.*)* Monsieur will be leaving us soon. I am sure he will forgive me if I say my farewells now.

DE TENDALE. Madame...

CÉLESTINE. Please, mammá... It's scarcely even dark. It's too early to go to bed. And I do so want to stay here with Léon.

LÉON. Yes, mammá. Let her stay...

MADAME DE VALOMBRE. Well, if you insist... *(To* CÉLESTINE.*)* But not too long now... *(Nodding to* DE TENDALE, VALOMBRE, *and* THE CURÉ.*)* If you will all excuse me...

VALOMBRE, *as* DE TENDALE *and* THE CURÉ *mumble their approval.* Of course, *chérie... (Kissing her hand without looking up, and almost without stopping his writing.)* Sleep well, my love.

THE CURÉ, *standing.* Madame...

> *She curtsies and exits, up right.* THE CURÉ *sits down again and resumes his nap.*

VALOMBRE, *to* LÉON, *holding up the letter.* Now, son, you say he came at you shouting. "You're a dead man!"...

LÉON. Yes, papá.

VALOMBRE. Good... Then I can seal it... I am sending the bailiff an exact account. A report of the whole incident... And I have asked the police commander for an escort too. At dawn, or even tonight, if possible, that villain and my letter will both be on their way to Cap-Français.

LÉON. So soon?

DE TENDALE, *to* VALOMBRE. Are you acting a trifle hastily, monsieur? Justice is best served by waiting at times. Surely it is a serious matter, but one ought to consider it closely, and from every—

VALOMBRE. Oh? And what would one see? A black runaway who comes back to murder my son... How complicated is that? Even if my heart were not demanding justice, the well-being of society would be pressing me to do so. In circumstances like these a public example is of the utmost good!

DE TENDALE. A public example? You assume that he is going to be condemned so quickly?

VALOMBRE. And why not? Tomorrow, tried, and the next day, hanged...

DE TENDALE. Ah, monsieur... Listen, I beg of you. In all seriousness, my friend... I understand a father's righteous anger. Who cannot feel within himself the seeds of such weakness?

VALOMBRE. Weakness?

DE TENDALE. But heed the language of reason, monsieur. You think that an example will be useful in the present circumstances?

VALOMBRE, *about to offer a vigorous reply.* I—

DE TENDALE, *interrupting.* Ah! It is precisely these circumstances that cause me to doubt it. To fear, rather, lest spirits, in utter frustration, be driven too far... One excess leads to another.

VALOMBRE. But justice, monsieur—

DE TENDALE. One must not fly in the face of the people!

VALOMBRE. The people? I beg your pardon! *(Angrily.)* A vicious monster, an assassin? A villain? We dare not punish him for fear of displeasing what you call "the people"?

DE TENDALE. Monsieur...

VALOMBRE. What? You have to let yourselves be killed, to be sure that "the people" don't rise up and kill you"?... A pretty philosophy, monsieur, I must say!

DE TENDALE, *trying to calm him.* Now, now... No one claims that their crimes should go unpunished. But with wise circumspection... And cautiously, monsieur... No violent sentences...

VALOMBRE. No violent—

DE TENDALE. Sometimes, and at times like these above all, we must be willing to close our eyes to many an offense...

VALOMBRE, *almost speechless.* We must—

DE TENDALE, *continuing.* ...lest we drive the people to despair, my friend... The people, after all, who have great strength... And who, for the most part, have right on their side.

VALOMBRE, *jumping to his feet, outraged.* Good God in heaven! "Right on their side"?

> *He begins pacing back and forth, stopping from time to time.*

DE TENDALE. "For the most part," I said... I fear you are not familiar with revolutions, monsieur. They force us to cast a veil over the shortcomings of the people. Over their every fault... But their will is the very soul of the nation...

VALOMBRE. Their will—

DE TENDALE. And when they rise up, the law, monsieur... That law, which one deems the mere expression of that will, must yield to it, in truth.

VALOMBRE, *stunned.* I... I...

DE TENDALE. If you would heed my opinion, monsieur... An opinion which, today, is no more than advice, but which shortly can have the force of authority at Cap-Français... If you would heed it, my friend, you would reject the idea of having that slave put to death, and would be satisfied merely to lock him up as a madman, a... a fugitive, monsieur... and render him incapable of harming the society. Myself, I shall take the appropriate governmental measures.

VALOMBRE, *stopping in front of him.* Say what you please, monsieur. *(Unable to control his anger.)* I'll be damned if I bother to answer!

CÉLESTINE, *clasping her hand to her mouth.* Papá!

LÉON, *standing up, to* VALOMBRE. Please, father. If I may have a word... I wanted to let monsieur have his say, because I feel as he does, though not for his reasons.

VALOMBRE. Oh?

LÉON. No power in the world, whatever the circumstance, should keep justice from being done. That is as it should be, as the law demands. And if danger is the result, then one needs all the more courage. Yes, so be it...

VALOMBRE. Indeed...

LÉON, *continuing.* But other concerns prevent me... *(To* DE TENDALE.) Justice, yes! Clearly it must be done, and I desire it! *(To* VALOMBRE.) But I must assure you, father... *(Pointing to* THE CURÉ.) And I trust *mon père* is listening...

THE CURÉ, *waking with a start.* Hmmph...

LÉON. I assure you that, if I were called as a witness, I would state that Timur... I would say that he acted like any other worthy gentleman... That he did what I would have done in his place...

VALOMBRE. You what?

LÉON. ...and that I surely cannot demand his death!

CÉLESTINE. Oh, brother dear! I don't know what makes you say that, but I'm sure that you are right.

VALOMBRE. Of all... Good God! Are they all losing their minds?... Léon... Haven't you caused enough grief today? Do you want to rob me of my only consolation?

THE CURÉ, *to* VALOMBRE. Monsieur Léon speaks from his charitable heart. He would pardon his assassin, as his Christian duty demands. What could be more fitting?

VALOMBRE. But—

THE CURÉ, *continuing.* But I do not believe, Monsieur de Valombre, that you are obliged to accept his opinion. Doubtless there are things in what he has said, and for whatever reasons, that I fail to comprehend. And I would take it upon myself to point out to him that there is no excuse for a man of honor attempting to do what this black man attempted.

VALOMBRE, *looking at* LÉON. Indeed!

THE CURÉ. And this one especially. He is all the more blameworthy in that he was not entirely ignorant of his sacred obligations. A number of times he came to church. I taught him what little I could. I even offered to marry him... Yes, to that black woman who was present at his crime...

VALOMBRE. That black woman? Ah! Of course! (*To* THE CURÉ.) Well, well, *mon père!* You see what all your fine words have produced! You talk marriage, and fidelity, and jealousy to these creatures, and you see what comes of it!

THE CURÉ. Your reproach would grieve me, monsieur, were it not baseless. Yes, I counseled fidelity to the blacks. But I beg you to recall that, at the same time, I preached chastity to the whites!

VALOMBRE. Yes... Yes... Well... And that is the problem. One expects the whites to be perfect, and one lets the blacks do as they wish. (*Enraged.*) Oh!... Leave me alone! (*Pointing to the door, down left.*) Out! Everyone!... Get out!

He sits down at the table.

LÉON, *as the others look at one another, uncertain what to do.* Please, father dear... Try to understand how unhappy it makes me to deny your ideas... How much it pains me to voice an opinion that might seem to stem from weakness... But I assure you that this is truly how I feel. Sincerely, father dear!... Oh! I have learned so much! So much, papá...

There is a long silence, during which VALOMBRE *sits staring at the floor as the others continue to look uneasily at one another.*

DE TENDALE, *clearing his throat.* Since no one seems to have anything to say... If I may... And because my position and my principles render me impartial... As I listened to you all, every manner of prejudice seemed to be standing before me. And in the arena where philosophy, as it were, was supreme. But the one clear fact that emerges from your debate is this: this poor black cannot be brought before the tribunal. That being so, Monsieur

de Valombre, kindly rip up your letter and accept the counsel
that reason and honor dictate!

VALOMBRE. Monsieur...

DE TENDALE. You who have power... Be merciful, I enjoin you. One
day the hearts of your blacks will find the way to show their
gratitude.

> *As he sits down in the armchair, down left,* MORIN *comes
> running in, down left, excitedly.*

MORIN, *to* VALOMBRE. Monsieur... Monsieur... Quick! They're
here!...

VALOMBRE. "They... "?

MORIN. I hardly had time to warn you...

VALOMBRE. What?

MORIN. Blacks, monsieur... A crowd... They met together and left
the settlement...

VALOMBRE. Who?

MORIN. I tried to stop them, but they wouldn't obey! They said
they want to talk to you... *(Pointing down left.)* They're right
behind me...

VALOMBRE, *troubled.* So?

LÉON. What do they want?

MORIN. I don't know! They wouldn't tell me... They wouldn't listen... But I think it's about the carpenter...

VALOMBRE, *to* DE TENDALE. The prisoner... *(To* LÉON.) What should
I do?

DE TENDALE. A redress of grievances, monsieur... A request... All perfectly in order... You should receive them and hear them out.

THE CURÉ, *standing up, to* VALOMBRE. I shall go talk to them, monsieur, if you wish.

LÉON. No, no, *mon père.* If anyone should go... I am the one concerned! It's an unfortunate precedent to set, but... *(Listening.)* Ah! I can hear them... *(Looking at* VALOMBRE *and* CÉLESTINE.) Another moment and they will be here... It's too late to resist...

    He turns to leave.

VALOMBRE, *standing up, center.* No, son! *(Seizing* LÉON's *arm.)* Send them in, Morin! I'm ready...

    MORIN *exits, down left.*

LÉON, *to* CÉLESTINE, *who is clearly quite distressed.* Leave, Célestine!... Please! I beg you...

CÉLESTINE, *firmly.* No, Léon!

    As she goes upstage, resolutely leaning against the mantelpiece, MORIN *comes running back in.*

MORIN, *to* VALOMBRE. Monsieur...

    A dozen blacks follow him in, take a few steps hesitantly approaching VALOMBRE, *still holding* LÉON's *arm, and stop.* THE CURÉ *is standing behind them.* DE TENDALE *is still in the armchair, down left. There is a heavy silence as the blacks shuffle about uneasily, each waiting for another to speak.*

VALOMBRE. Well?

JUAN, *who is in front of the group.* We want... We want...

    He stops.

JEAN-PIERRE, *at the back of the group.* Timur! We want Timur!

    The other blacks mutter their agreement: "Yes, Timur...," "We want Timur...," "We want him...," etc.

VALOMBRE. Oh? And by what right?

    There is another heavy silence.

JEAN-PIERRE. Timur...

    The others, mumbling, echo the name.

VALOMBRE. Your Timur ran away... And your Timur tried to kill his master! He is in prison, and he will be judged! One cannot hand him over to you. Nor would I if I were able.

JEAN-PIERRE. Timur...

    The others echo the name, though with less conviction.

VALOMBRE. I repeat. It is not possible. He stands accused of a crime. He must be judged. And he shall be!

JEAN-PIERRE. But... We want Timur.

JUAN. Yes! We want him! We want him!

VALOMBRE. You have no right to demand him, nor have I the right to hand him over. You were wrong to come here. I pardon you this time... But do so again and I assure you... Your punishment will be severe! *(Pointing down left.)* Now leave! All of you!

JEAN-PIERRE. But... Timur...

VALOMBRE. Silence!... Now leave! *(The blacks look at one another, hesitating, and retreat timidly as he takes a menacing step toward them.)* You hear me? Next time you will be punished, as you deserve! *(Pointing.)* Now, out!

MORIN, *pushing them.* Out!... Out!

> *The blacks slowly leave, muttering under their breath: "But, Timur...," "We want Timur...," "We thought...," etc.* JEAN-PIERRE *is the last to leave. He casts a vicious glance at* VALOMBRE *but lowers his eyes as the latter stands his ground and returns his gaze sternly.* MORIN *follows him out.*

LÉON, *embracing* VALOMBRE. Papá...

> CÉLESTINE *joins them, takes* VALOMBRE's *hand and kisses it. They stand together, in silence, for a long moment.*

THE CURÉ. Poor children!

> *He withdraws, up right, as* MORIN *returns.*

MORIN, *to* VALOMBRE. No sooner were they outside, monsieur, than all of them left, as fast as they could.

VALOMBRE. Keep an eye on them, Morin. And carefully, understand? But no punishment. Not this time... No punishment, you hear?

> CÉLESTINE *returns to the fireplace.*

DE TENDALE, *standing up, holding out his hand to* VALOMBRE. My compliments, monsieur. *(Shaking his hand.)* Firmness tempered with gentleness... Not one without the other! The saving grace of power, my friend!

VALOMBRE. Yes, well... (*To* LÉON.) So far, so good. For now at least... They will send him off tonight. He will be judged as a runaway if not as a murderer. And tomorrow will be the end of it.

LÉON. For your sake, papá, let us hope...

DE TENDALE. One moment, my friends... Thus far I agree with everything you say and do. (*To* VALOMBRE.) Your conduct, monsieur, has been irreproachable. Every request, after all, must be heard. (*To* LÉON.) And he has heard theirs. But every request must also be well founded and in keeping with the law. Theirs was not, and he has rejected it. Precisely as he should have done... (*To* VALOMBRE.) But now, monsieur, prudence must come to the fore.

VALOMBRE. Monsieur?

DE TENDALE, *continuing*. True, you have refused their demand, founded on no legal basis. Now, wisdom demands that you grant it. Freely, and of your own accord.

VALOMBRE. That I—

DE TENDALE. In so doing you will calm their spirits and, at the same time, gain their confidence and respect. It will be a gesture both equitable and clever.

VALOMBRE. You mean... I resisted when there was danger, but I should agree when there is none?

LÉON, *to* VALOMBRE. No, no, father! Don't listen... You must be firm. Prudence goes hand in hand with determination!

DE TENDALE. My young friend...

LÉON, *continuing*. One moment of weakness will give rise to others. We shall only encourage such traitorous gatherings if we show that they bear fruit... No, no! You must announce tomorrow that any similar actions are expressly forbidden, and that the punishment will be severe. Order must be maintained at all costs, however harsh. To retreat would be clumsy and cowardly!

VALOMBRE. Léon...

DE TENDALE, *to* LÉON. Ah, monsieur... Your maxims of individual honor are quite out of place in a commerce such as yours. What's more, that honor is no more than a personal prejudice, a bias... What shame is there in yielding to the people's will? It is with gradual concessions that one disarms the people. That is how revolutions have always proceeded, as I daresay you can see!

LÉON. Yes, I see, monsieur! I see many things... And I judge them more clearly now! I see that, when authority is flouted, anarchy is the result.

DE TENDALE. Ah! Finally, that big word!... Anarchy...

VALOMBRE. Monsieur...

DE TENDALE. Let tyranny show the slightest weakening, and what do they call it? Anarchy!

LÉON. Were we tyrants, monsieur? *(Sarcastically.)* I must say, I didn't know!... But be that as it may, our situation has grown simpler now. We are at war with the enemy.

DE TENDALE. War, my young friend? You forget who stands before you! You forget my authority.

VALOMBRE. Monsieur...

DE TENDALE. Do you think you are without defenses? Will the fatherland abandon you? Does the Assemblée nationale not take you under its wing and protect you? Trust me, messieurs. I shall take everything in hand. When I return to Cap-Français I shall request an audience with the governor. I shall take steps, my friends. In less than two days I shall publish a proclamation.

LÉON. A proclamation?

VALOMBRE, *sarcastically.* Balm for our wounds!

LÉON, *to* DE TENDALE. A... Are you serious, monsieur? A proclamation? Can the blacks even read?

DE TENDALE. And whose fault is that?... But please, no recriminations... Trust me, I tell you. I shall see to everything. You have read my instructions...

VALOMBRE. Truly, monsieur... I appreciate... We thank you... But God in heaven! What could you do if... if...

DE TENDALE. If?

VALOMBRE. If the worst...

LÉON, *to* DE TENDALE. Yes, what?

DE TENDALE. What? Why, it is as I say, messieurs. My authority is absolute. I am leaving... But after tomorrow you shall learn what I can do.

VALOMBRE, *with a respectful little bow. Au revoir*, monsieur. And may heaven protect you.

LÉON, *to* VALOMBRE, *under his breath.* At least now we'll be free.

DE TENDALE, *overhearing, to* LÉON. Yes, free... No doubt... Free to act on your philosophy, my young friend...

LÉON. Monsieur...

DE TENDALE. But sooner or later the revolution will be victorious.

LÉON, *snapping his fingers.* A... A fig for your revolution!

VALOMBRE. Léon!

LÉON. Things were going perfectly well just as they were.

DE TENDALE. Come, come now... Let us not be discouraged. I assure you... *(Getting ready to leave.)* But it is growing late. The horses are waiting... Adieu, messieurs... Once again I beg of you. Let there be no violence. No imprudent measures. Give me time to act. You need have no fear. Should the situation become too embroiled, I shall write to Monsieur Barnave.[1]

VALOMBRE, *under his breath, to* LÉON. Much good that will do!

DE TENDALE, *overhearing.* Indeed, monsieur! The most influential member of the Assemblée for colonial affairs...

VALOMBRE, *unimpressed.* Aha...

DE TENDALE. But I must be on my way... *(Approaching the door, down left, nodding to* CÉLESTINE.*)* Mademoiselle... *(To* VALOMBRE *and* LÉON.*)* Messieurs...

He gives a silent nod to THE CURÉ.

VALOMBRE, *following him.* Let me see you out.

DE TENDALE. No need, my friend... Adieu... And remember that, as Robespierre told us, principles must always be the last to perish.[2]

VALOMBRE. Principles? The last? *(Returning.)* And what of us?

DE TENDALE *exits.*

1. Antoine Barnave was deputy to the Assemblée nationale and a member of the Committee on the Colonies.
2. "Les principes doivent périr les derniers" are the famous words of Robespierre, an outspoken leader in the period of the French Revolution commonly known as the Reign of Terror, which ended with his arrest and execution in 1794.

LÉON. Gone! *(Joining* VALOMBRE, *center.)* We are the masters now, papá.

VALOMBRE. Did you hear? Principles must always be the last... A fine principle, that!... Well?

LÉON. "Well," papá?

VALOMBRE. What do you think of your revolution now?

LÉON. It... It isn't precisely what I was hoping for.

VALOMBRE. You thought that, with all my wisdom, my care, I was only an old babbler!

LÉON. Not at all, papá! That's not what I thought!... Besides, even if... No, no... Let me tend to our affairs. Say what he will, you must hold Timur.

VALOMBRE. We agree on that, Léon! *(To* THE CURÉ, *still up right.)* What do you think, *mon père?*

THE CURÉ. In cases as difficult as these, monsieur, one must leave matters as they are and trust in the ways of almighty Providence.

> GALAOR *comes running in, down left.*

GALAOR, *to* VALOMBRE, *stammering excitedly.* Master!... Morin can't come himself... He wants me to tell you... He wants me to tell monsieur that he doesn't know what to do...

VALOMBRE. Galaor?

GALAOR. He wanted to give Jean-Pierre a little flogging and have him put in irons. But the blacks began crowding around and shouting "Timur... Timur... " He thinks they're going to try to free him.

CÉLESTINE, *coming center, to* LÉON. Oh! What now, brother dear?

LÉON. Good God!

VALOMBRE, *to* GALAOR. Are they coming here?

THE CURÉ. Let me go see, monsieur.

He crosses himself and exits, down left.

LÉON, *to* VALOMBRE. Please, let me take care of it! *(Calling.)* Jean-Jacques! *(To* VALOMBRE.) This time I insist! It's my turn!

CÉLESTINE. Léon... Brother dear...

LÉON, *calling.* Jean-Jacques!

A moment later JEAN-JACQUES *enters, down left.*

JEAN-JACQUES. Monsieur?

LÉON. My pistols, Jean-Jacques!... And you... Take your rifle!

JEAN-JACQUES. Yes, master.

LÉON. Can I count on you, my friend?

JEAN-JACQUES. Oh yes! Yes, master dear...

He exits, down left.

VALOMBRE, *to* LÉON. Don't leave... We have to stay together...

ROSINE *comes running in, down left, breathless.*

ROSINE, *to* VALOMBRE. Oh! Master...

VALOMBRE. Rosine?

ROSINE. Help! Help! They're coming...

CÉLESTINE, *about to panic.* Oh... Léon...

ROSINE. God save us!

LÉON. My pistols!... *(Calling.)* Jean-Jacques!

VALOMBRE, *to* LÉON. Your mother, Léon...

LÉON, *pointing up right.* Quick! Go to her!

CÉLESTINE. Mammá...

THE CURÉ *enters, down left, in obvious distress.*

LÉON, *to* THE CURÉ. *Mon père?*

THE CURÉ. Ah! I saw... I saw...

VALOMBRE. What?

THE CURÉ. All of them... Coming this way... *(He crosses himself.)* And armed...

LÉON, *shouting.* Jean-Jacques!

VALOMBRE. Where is Morin? *(To* THE CURÉ.) Call Morin!

THE CURÉ. No use, monsieur! Jean-Pierre... Just now... He was carrying his head on a sugarcane stalk![3] I saw...

There is a moment of consternation and shock.

VALOMBRE, *as* THE CURÉ *continues to cross himself.* God help us!

CÉLESTINE. Oh...

---

3. The practice of displaying heads on sticks during the storming of the Bastille in France was duplicated by rebelling slaves during the Haitian revolution.

LÉON, *shouting.* Jean-Jacques!

    CÉLESTINE *falls in a faint at his feet.* MARIE-LOUISE *comes running in, up right.*

MARIE-LOUISE, *shouting.* Fire! Fire! *(To* VALOMBRE.*)* Oh! Master dear!

VALOMBRE, *noticing* CÉLESTINE. Célestine...

MARIE-LOUISE. Help! Save madame! *(Pointing up right.)* It's burning, monsieur!

VALOMBRE, *pointing to* CÉLESTINE. Help her, Léon! *(Running to the door, up right.)* Your mother... I must save your mother!

    He dashes out, followed by THE CURÉ, *leaving the door open.*

LÉON. And no pistols, damn it!

MARIE-LOUISE, *bending over* CÉLESTINE. Mademoiselle!... Dear child...

    LÉON *lifts* CÉLESTINE *onto his shoulders. Just then, a group of blacks burst in, down left, pushing aside* GALAOR, *still standing by the door, shaken. They are led by* JEAN-JACQUES, *brandishing two pistols.*

JEAN-JACQUES, *to the blacks.* He's here... I'm sure... *(Pointing to* LÉON *with one of the pistols.)* See?

LÉON. Ah! Jean-Jacques! My pistols...

JEAN-JACQUES. Here! For you...

    He aims the pistol at him.

GALAOR. No!

JEAN-JACQUES. Die... (*sarcastically*) ...master!

As he fires, GALAOR *jumps in front of* LÉON.

GALAOR. Master dear...

He takes the shot and falls dead at LÉON's *feet.*

LÉON, *to* JEAN-JACQUES, *in shock and rage.* Traitor! (*Holding* CÉLES-
TINE *against his body.*) Go on! Kill us both! You swine!

As JEAN-JACQUES *loads the other pistol,* TIMUR *comes running
in, down left, his left arm bandaged and a hatchet in his right.
Before* JEAN-JACQUES *can shoot,* TIMUR *gives his hand a violent
blow, disarming him. One can see the flickering of the flames
through the open door, up right.*

TIMUR. No, no!

JEAN-JACQUES. Timur!

TIMUR. The white man is mine!

LÉON. Take your revenge, Timur! You and you alone have the right!

TIMUR. My revenge? Oh yes, I will, I assure you! But not just yet...
So! Who is the master now, white dog?

He heaves a contented sigh.

LÉON. Then kill me, damn it! Kill me or let me go!

TIMUR. Neither one, I'm afraid! (*To several blacks.*) Tie up our dear
master!

LÉON. You would dare take my sister from me?

TIMUR. Have no fear! I want her alive!

    LÉON *is bound as one of the blacks takes* CÉLESTINE *and carries her unceremoniously under his arm.*

MARIE-LOUISE, *to the inert* CÉLESTINE. Mademoiselle!... My child... Speak to me... Speak to me...

LÉON, *to* TIMUR. And my parents?

    The flashes from the fire become brighter and brighter.

TIMUR. They are none of my concern.

    JEAN-PIERRE, JUAN, ALMANZOR, TÉLÉMAQUE, *and the other blacks enter, down left.*

JEAN-PIERRE. Timur...

TIMUR. Ah, there you are... Is it done?

JEAN-PIERRE. One, two, three...

LÉON. And my father?

JEAN-PIERRE. Killed... See?

    He points to JUAN, *who is wearing* VALOMBRE'*s bloody frockcoat.*

LÉON. And my mother?

JEAN-PIERRE, *very matter-of-fact.* Burned to a crisp.

LÉON, *covering his face.* God help us!

TIMUR, *to* JEAN-PIERRE. Is that all? Are you finished?

JEAN-PIERRE. I think so. And you?

ALMANZOR. When do we have supper?

JEAN-PIERRE. Supper? It's all burning...

TÉLÉMAQUE. Tsk tsk tsk!

TIMUR. Who set the fire?

JEAN-PIERRE. I did.

TIMUR. Why?

JEAN-PIERRE. For fun, Timur! What else?

TIMUR, *shaking his head.* Come... Our work here is done.

JEAN-PIERRE. All done!

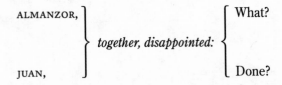

ALMANZOR,
JUAN,   *together, disappointed:*   What?   Done?

TÉLÉMAQUE. You mean, that's all there is?

JUAN, *pointing to* LÉON *and* CÉLESTINE, *moving toward them.* We still have our fine feathered friends to—

TIMUR, *stepping in front of him.* Stop! Those two are mine!

JEAN-PIERRE. Oh no! They're mine, Timur!

JEAN-JACQUES, *pointing to* LÉON. That one is mine! (*To* LÉON.) Right, master?

They approach LÉON *menacingly.*

TIMUR, *brandishing his hatchet.* One more step and I swear...

JUAN. Timur!

ALMANZOR. Enough, you two... He's Timur's... He's the one to kill him!

TÉLÉMAQUE. You're right! Absolutely...

JEAN-PIERRE, *to* TIMUR. Then kill him and be done with it!

ALMANZOR. Kill him!

JUAN. Kill him!

TÉLÉMAQUE, *nodding.* Kill him!

TIMUR. When it suits me, my friends... All in good time... Now shut your mouths!

The glow from the flames offstage grows brighter.

JEAN-PIERRE. Kill him, damn it!

The rest of the blacks, milling about upstage, begin echoing "Kill him!" but a moment later their cries turn to "Fire! Fire!" as they point up right.

TIMUR, *in the ensuing turmoil.* Out! All of you! *(Pointing down left.)* Out! Out!! *(To one of the blacks, pointing to* LÉON.) You... You're in charge of this one! Understand?

MARIE-LOUISE, *softly, as* TIMUR *takes* CÉLESTINE *from the black holding her.* Mademoiselle... Oh, mistress dear...

TIMUR, *to himself, as the others all exit frantically, down left, as best they can.* What's done is done... No more... At least we are free! *(At the door, about to exit.)* Now to find Badia...

MARIE-LOUISE *falls in a heap, reaching out to* CÉLESTINE *as* TIMUR *carries her off.*

End of Act IV

ACT V

A wide expanse by the sea, with a small hill upstage overlooking the water, a clump of trees at its feet and other trees here and there. In the distance can be seen the smoking ruins of the plantation, and others, likewise smoldering, dotting the landscape as far as the horizon.

At rise, day is dawning. Juan, Almanzor, Télémaque, Jean-Pierre, and the other blacks, all carrying sticks, are sitting and lying about on the ground, most of them upstage, at the foot of the hill. Léon and Célestine are bound back to back, upstage, under guard. The Curé, wrists bound, is upstage, partly concealed behind several blacks. Downstage, Timur is seated on the ground beneath a coconut tree. Hélène is kneeling beside him tending to his wounded arm.

HÉLÈNE. Does it pain you, love?

TIMUR. No, Badia. Not really...

HÉLÈNE. But you are so quiet. And you seem so sad.

TIMUR. It's just... I was thinking... Thinking... *(After a pause.)* What now, Badia? What will we do?

HÉLÈNE. Do, Touko?... We are free... And together, you and I...

TIMUR. Yes. *You* are free. That gives me hope. Free and safe... Free from their attacks, their insults! Oh Badia! Even if only for you alone... *(He moves to kiss her but stops abruptly.)* No... *(Pushing her away, shaking his head.)* No...

HÉLÈNE. Touko! Touko!... What is it? Why... *(He turns his head aside.)* It... It wasn't my fault. I... He...

TIMUR. I know. It was the white man's fault! All of slavery's fault! The fault of everything that is finished now... Over and done... But everything that was... That was, Badia... (HÉLÈNE *hangs her head as he casts a look at* LÉON.) The monster! The savage!... See how he weeps!

HÉLÈNE. Touko!

TIMUR. What?

HÉLÈNE, *plaintively.* Will you never kiss me again? Never touch me...

TIMUR. No... Not until I am avenged...

HÉLÈNE. But... You are, love! You are!

TIMUR. Oh? The blacks are avenged. But me?

HÉLÈNE. Then what do you want to do? How will you—

TIMUR. Want? I... *(After a thoughtful pause.)* We shall see... Yes, we shall see.

HÉLÈNE. I'm frightened, Touko!

TIMUR. What for? For him? *(Pointing to* LÉON.) For that one?

HÉLÈNE. No, Touko! For you! You seem so angry. So unhappy...

TIMUR. Hear me out, Badia. We have not seen the end of it. What now? What do we do? Go live in the forest? We could have fled there without rebelling... Idle our days away on this ravaged earth? We are not in Africa, Badia. In Africa, content with nothing to do... Here, we must work. But how? Who knows?

HÉLÈNE. Touko...

TIMUR, *continuing.* Besides, there are still whites. They can come back at any time. Our few guns are no match... And we have no leader. No leader...

HÉLÈNE, *objecting.* But you...

TIMUR. Oh yes, I know. I am their leader. But what kind of leader? A leader who has no idea what to do, where to begin... No idea which way to turn... And yet my idea was so good, Badia. *(Musing.)* So good, so well planned... *(Sighing.)* No... It is not easy to be free!

HÉLÈNE. Oh, Touko! If only we had a boat. A little one even... To go back home...

TIMUR, *shaking his head.* Poor Badia!...

HÉLÈNE. To Africa...

TIMUR. Yes, my idea was so good. There were three of them and... *(looking toward the blacks)* ...and all of us! It made such good sense.

HÉLÈNE. But before, Touko... Long ago... Did the whites have guns then? And uniforms, and leaders? Was it always like that?

TIMUR. Of course! They were white! And they came from Europe, where everything is possible. But here? Here, Badia? Nothing is clear. Everything is confused... Still, my idea was so good.

The blacks upstage begin to stir.

JUAN, *jovially.* To work, Timur! It's daylight, and there's work to be done! *(The other blacks give good-natured little laughs.)* Remember what Morin used to say!

TÉLÉMAQUE. Ha!

The blacks mumble their displeasure at the name: "Oh, Morin...," "Damn him!" "No more, no more...," etc.

JUAN. Ah, what a pleasure to have nothing to do. No work...

TIMUR. Oh? Nothing? Are you sure?

JUAN. Of course. Who for?

TIMUR. For yourself!

JUAN. But I don't like sugar.

TÉLÉMAQUE. I do! I do!

JUAN, *to* TÉLÉMAQUE. Then go make some!

TÉLÉMAQUE. Ha ha! I'd rather not!

TIMUR, *to* TÉLÉMAQUE. Then how will you get it?

TÉLÉMAQUE. I'll go take it.

TIMUR. From... ?

TÉLÉMAQUE. From... From the merchants in town.

TIMUR. And who is going to make it for them? *(Pointing to the blacks.)* Will they? Will you?

TÉLÉMAQUE. Oh no!

TIMUR. Well?

TÉLÉMAQUE. I don't care who makes it. I want sugar, that's all...

ALMANZOR, *who has been listening, to* TIMUR. What if we put the whites to work?

TIMUR. Oh? Which ones?

ALMANZOR. Well... I...

JUAN, *pointing to* LÉON. Why not that one?

ALMANZOR. I'll go get him a pick. He can start now!

TIMUR, *sternly.* I told you all not to touch him!

JUAN. And the prisoner? The other one?

TIMUR. Who? What prisoner?

JUAN. Jean-Pierre's... The one he took at the plantation yesterday... The one he didn't kill...

ALMANZOR. Good idea...

TIMUR. Oh? *(To* JEAN-PIERRE.) Jean-Pierre... Bring us your white.

JEAN-PIERRE. Why? He's mine.

TIMUR. Who is it?

JEAN-PIERRE. Wait... I'll show you... *(He gestures to some of the blacks upstage.)* Bring the dog here!

Two of the blacks lead THE CURÉ, *wrists bound, downstage.*

TIMUR, *taken aback.* What? Him? Who told you... Free him!

JEAN-PIERRE. What?

TIMUR. Free him, I said!

JEAN-PIERRE. I beg your pardon! He's my prisoner. Mine...

TIMUR. Yours? And what are you going to do with him?

JEAN-PIERRE. What business is it—

TIMUR. Not kill him, I hope...

JEAN-PIERRE. Oh?

TIMUR. If you dared... If you so much as—

JEAN-PIERRE. If...?

TIMUR. Enough! I'm ordering you...

JEAN-PIERRE. Ordering? My, my... You're talking like a white man!

TIMUR. I'm talking like a man, Jean-Pierre. Not an animal, like you...

THE CURÉ, *to* TIMUR. Thank you, monsieur... But you need not be concerned for me. I am very old. What have I left to lose? But I beg you... (*Pointing to* LÉON *and* CÉLESTINE.) These two poor orphans... Please, monsieur... Free them from their bonds.

TIMUR. Be still!... You, in that black skirt of yours! Their fate is decided.

HÉLÈNE. Touko... This white was always kind. Remember how good he used to be to us? How he wanted us to marry, just like the whites? How he told you always to love no one but me?

TIMUR. I know... I know...

HÉLÈNE. Please...

TIMUR, *to the two blacks holding* THE CURÉ. Free him!

> *A number of the blacks shout their disapproval: "No!" "He's a white man!" "Kill him, kill him!" etc.*

JEAN-PIERRE. If I were you, Timur... (*He mimes slitting his throat.*) And the sooner the better!

> *The blacks continue shouting.*

TIMUR. Quiet! All of you!... You remember how we used to go to his church sometimes? How he used to give us wine on Sundays?

TÉLÉMAQUE, *enthusiastically.* Oh yes!

ALMANZOR. That's true... I suppose... But—

> *The blacks react with mumbled approval: "Yes, that's true!"*
> *"He gave us wine...," etc.*

TIMUR. So, we keep him. We must not kill him! Understand?

JEAN-PIERRE, *under his breath.* Bah!

TIMUR. He can make every day a Sunday for us!

TÉLÉMAQUE. Wine? Every day?

> *The blacks continue their muttered approval: "Good idea!"*
> *"Let's keep him!" etc.*

TIMUR, *to* THE CURÉ, *as he is freed from his bonds, in a whisper.* Peace, monsieur...

JUAN, *to* JEAN-PIERRE, *in a whisper.* What good is our opinion? Timur does as he pleases.

JEAN-PIERRE, *replying in a whisper.* He always had a weakness for the whites. If you ask me...

TIMUR, *addressing the blacks.* My brothers... Now, finally, you are free. But if you wish to remain free, we will still have to work.

TÉLÉMAQUE. Work?

TIMUR. Yes. But for ourselves... For our own salvation... Do you think the whites sit and do nothing all the livelong day?

JEAN-PIERRE, *to* JUAN, *in a whisper.* You see? The whites...

TIMUR, *continuing.* Look at their port... Their strongholds, their ships... Work is everywhere. If we would be victorious, we must do as they do.

JUAN, *to* JEAN-PIERRE, *in a whisper.* You hear?

TIMUR, *continuing.* They can still attack us. The constables, the militia... The garrison... Yes, we must be on guard. Jean-Pierre will go scouting along the northern plain, and I will go over the road to Cap-Français... The rest of you will keep watch here. Beware of any armed men, any riders on horseback. You must not let them pass! Be brave, my brothers! A few days of cour-' age, and we will be able to sleep in peace.

JEAN-PIERRE. Very well, Timur. Only remember... (*Pointing to* LÉON.) You promised to kill that vicious white. *(Scornfully.)* The young master... And we expect you to keep your word.

TIMUR. Trust me. (*With a knowing glance at* HÉLÈNE.) I have more to avenge than all of you! But first, our safety... Security above all... (*To* JEAN-PIERRE.) Are you ready to leave? (JEAN-PIERRE *nods.*) Good. Take several men with you. And your rifle... Now, who will come with me?

Several blacks stand up.

JUAN, *to* TIMUR. What do we do with the prisoners?

TIMUR. You and Zozor... Tie them to the coconut tree. *(With a little laugh, pointing to* THE CURÉ, *standing by the tree.)* They can talk to monsieur. That should please them. (*To* THE CURÉ.) When your people are going to die, they talk to someone in a skirt. Right?

THE CURÉ. Alas!

TIMUR. You see? I know the white man's religion!

HÉLÈNE, *to* TIMUR. Touko, take me with you.

TIMUR. Why?

HÉLÈNE, *pointing to* LÉON. I can't stand to look at him. Please, Touko... Please...

TIMUR. Very well... Come along... *(To* ALMANZOR *and* JUAN.*)* I am leaving you two to guard the prisoners. All three are in your hands.

As he and HÉLÈNE *exit, right, with several blacks,* CLOTILDE, HERMIONE, MARIE-LOUISE, *and* VÉNUS *enter, up left, and watch them leave.*

JEAN-PIERRE, *to* JUAN, *in a whisper.* We have work to do, my friend! I'll talk to you later. *(To the several blacks accompanying him.)* Come...

They exit, down left.

CLOTILDE, *to* HERMIONE *and* VÉNUS. My, my... She and Timur are back together, I see!

VÉNUS. So it seems...

HERMIONE, *with a nod toward* LÉON. Now that her white lover is a prisoner! Of course!

VÉNUS. She's a clever one, she is.

ALMANZOR *brings* LÉON *and* CÉLESTINE *downstage. He and* JUAN *tie them to the coconut tree.*

MARIE-LOUISE, *leaving the other three women, up left, and throwing herself at* CÉLESTINE's *feet.* Oh, mistress dear!... Mademoiselle... My child...

She embraces her ankles.

CÉLESTINE, *with a shriek of terror.* Ayyy!... A snake! Kill it, Léon! Kill it!... It's biting my foot!

MARIE-LOUISE. Oh, mademoiselle... Don't you know me?... Dear God! Your nurse... Your nurse... The only mother you have now, mademoiselle...

CÉLESTINE, *raving.* My mother?... Mammá?... You? Mammá?... But... But why are you so black? *(Groaning in pain.)* Oh...

MARIE-LOUISE. My child...

She remains crouching at her feet, disconsolate.

LÉON, *shaking his head.* Mad, poor thing... But it's better, God knows!

JEAN-JACQUES *enters, right, and strides boldly up to* LÉON.

JEAN-JACQUES. Ah! There you are... *(Sarcastically.)* Master!

LÉON. You?

JEAN-JACQUES. My coat, young man! It needs a good brushing!

LÉON. Spare me, you traitor!

JEAN-JACQUES. And if my horse isn't saddled in five minutes, a hundred lashes!

LÉON. God damn you to hell!

THE CURÉ, *to* LÉON. Please, monsieur! You must not add sin to the other woes you suffer. You must not curse your enemy. You must turn the other cheek, and love him...

LÉON, *to* JEAN-JACQUES. Of course! *(Hypocritically.)* Ah! You, my dear, dear friend? *(Breaking into tears.)* How happy I am to see you!

JEAN-JACQUES. Weep, crocodile!

He snaps his fingers in LÉON's *face and withdraws among the blacks.*

ALMANZOR, *to* LÉON. Quiet, you! *(Pointing his stick at* THE CURÉ, *who is holding out the crucifix about his neck toward* LÉON *and* CÉLESTINE.)* Look at that one! He's going to do his Sunday tricks!

THE CURÉ, *to* LÉON. Monsieur...

ALMANZOR, *to* JUAN. Watch him! He'll make you laugh!

THE CURÉ, *to* CÉLESTINE. And you, mademoiselle... In the name of the Lord, listen, I pray you...

ALMANZOR. Like at the church...

THE CURÉ, *continuing.* I would speak to you of your duty. May my words comfort and console you. You know the danger that besets you, my children. Think of yourselves and of your Lord. Implore his mercy. How dearly you both deserve it!

CÉLESTINE, *to* LÉON. What did he say, brother dear? What did the nice man tell me to do?

LÉON. He... Célestine...

CÉLESTINE, *to* MARIE-LOUISE, *still crouching at her feet.* I only want to catch that butterfly, mammá...

LÉON, *to* THE CURÉ. *Mon père... Mon père...* Her mind...

CÉLESTINE, *pointing in the air.* That one... See?

LÉON. My God! How it pains me to see her this way! I know she is suffering less, but still—

CÉLESTINE. Please, let me run after it... *(Pausing briefly, as if listening.)* A cold?... No, no... I won't, mammá! Believe me!... *(Pausing.)* But why not? Oh... *(Bursting into tears.)* Why not? Why not?

LÉON, *to* THE CURÉ. It breaks my heart.

THE CURÉ. Be strong, monsieur.

LÉON. If she knew... How much more would she weep, *mon père!*

THE CURÉ. Providence is kind. The disorder that it wreaks upon your poor sister's wits softens the horror of this unspeakable moment. It proves to us all that, after a life so blameless... A life so pure... She needs no meditation, no prayerful retreat to appear before God.

LÉON, *sighing*. Oh...

THE CURÉ. But you and I, monsieur Léon... We, whose reason remains intact... Is it not so that we may delve deep within ourselves and deserve divine pardon by repenting of our lives?

LÉON. Ah, *mon père!* In such chaos, how can I know what I feel? How can I know what I believe? It seems to me... Yes, it seems to me that, until this moment, your ideas were not mine...

THE CURÉ, *nodding*. I know... I know...

LÉON. But now I am not sure. In this one long day my mind has come undone! If bitter repentance is all I need to gain the joys of heaven... Ah, *mon père*... My soul is ready. All my lifelong habits, all my childhood ideas... Everything... Everything is in such confusion, turned upside down. I doubt my reason, I doubt my conscience... Good and evil? I no longer know which one is which... Truth? Falsehood?... Sin?

THE CURÉ. My child...

LÉON, *continuing*. I only know that I loathe the past. Oh! If only I could be happy today! How well I would know how to live my life! To live... To have a future... Oh! How I would redeem it all!... But no... I must die! I must, and I will... Oh! To die... To forget my past, forget my deeds... Forget my suffering... Yes, let me die, let me die... Let me cease to exist... I must...

THE CURÉ. Yes. Die you will... But cease to exist? No... No, you may not hope for that, monsieur. You must be strong... Strong enough to repent from this moment on... With no need to exist in this world, my son, or to cease to exist in the next!

JUAN, *who has been listening to* THE CURÉ, *scowling, to* ALMANZOR. What is all this, Zozor? (*Pointing to* THE CURÉ.) You said that one would make me laugh. But I'm listening and listening, and I'll be damned if he's very funny!

ALMANZOR. That's because he's not doing his Sunday tricks! (*To* THE CURÉ.) Listen, you. Sing for us a little. Like you always do.

JUAN. Yes!

TÉLÉMAQUE. That's right! Sing!

JUAN. Sing, you hear?

THE CURÉ. Dear Lord... (*Joining his hands in prayer.*) Might their commands be an echo of thy goodness? A reminder to intone thy holy words? (*To* LÉON.) Listen, my son, and join me in my heartfelt prayers. (*Chanting.*) Memento mori...

JUAN. That's better...

THE CURÉ, *continuing. In omnibus operibus tuis memorare novissima tua, et in aeternum non peccabis...*

The other blacks raise approving shouts: "That's right, sing!" "Hurrah, white man!" etc.

ALMANZOR. Good! Now do the other things. You know... All the magic... With the glass of wine and the little bits of bread...

THE CURÉ, *aghast.* What? Consecrate the host?

ALMANZOR. Whatever...

TÉLÉMAQUE. Like in the spring, with all the food!

THE CURÉ, *under his breath.* The Easter mass...

TÉLÉMAQUE. And we'll all kneel down, and you'll put bread in our mouths!

THE CURÉ. Oh! Make sport of the holy communion?

ALMANZOR. Yes! Do it! Go on! (*To* JUAN.) You'll see!

THE CURÉ. No! Certainly not!

JUAN. What do you mean, "No!" Go on, he said!

THE CURÉ. Never!

ALMANZOR, *raising his stick.* Hurry up, white man! On your knees! We're waiting!

LÉON, *to* THE CURÉ. Do what they say, *mon père.* What difference—

THE CURÉ. Oh? Profane a sacred miracle to amuse these idolaters? I would sooner die!

ALMANZOR, *seizing him by the throat.* Enough, you! How much longer—

THE CURÉ. Never... Never...

JUAN, *to* THE CURÉ. You dare say no to us? (*Seizing him by the wrists and shaking him.*) To us?

THE CURÉ, *as* ALMANZOR *also shakes him.* I... But...

LÉON. Please, *mon père...* I beg you...

CÉLESTINE. What game are they playing?

MARIE-LOUISE, *to* CÉLESTINE, *still at her feet.* There, there, my child...

ALMANZOR. He's asking to be whipped!

The blacks, in a frenzy, cry out: "The whip!" "Yes, the whip!" "Yes, yes!" etc.

JUAN, *pointing right.* Let's take him over there. We'll make him run the gauntlet and beat him till he drops!

The blacks agree with shouts of "Yes, yes!" "Till he drops!" etc.

LÉON, *to* THE CURÉ. *Mon père...*

THE CURÉ. God's will be done!

ALMANZOR, *dragging him by the cord around his wrists.* Come, you!

LÉON. Stop! You beasts!

THE CURÉ. Blessèd be, my children... Adieu... Pray for me!

ALMANZOR and JUAN drag him off, right.

LÉON. O horror of horrors!

CÉLESTINE. Brother dear, is it his turn to hide? Shall we all go seek?

LÉON, *in despair.* How much more...

MARIE-LOUISE, *to* CÉLESTINE. O my child... My poor child...

LÉON. What terrors can still be left?

He turns aside.

MARIE-LOUISE, *continuing.* Give me a little laugh, mademoiselle. Like when you were nursing, and I would tell you... And you would smile for me...

HERMIONE, *to* CLOTILDE. Did you see? Jean-Pierre is angry with Timur...

VÉNUS. To say the least... He's furious.

CLOTILDE. Why, I wonder?

LÉON, *softly, to himself, as the women continue.* Dear God! End my woe...

> *He stands, head hung low, oblivious to what is going on around him.*

HERMIONE. I heard him tell Timur he was just like the whites. That he wants to be the master...

VÉNUS. Maybe so...

> *A sharp cry is heard coming from offstage, right. The three women turn to look as the cries continue.*

CLOTILDE. Oh!

HERMIONE. The priest... Juan...

VÉNUS. Juan stabbed him!

CLOTILDE. He...

HERMIONE. He did!

VÉNUS. Oh my... Did you ever...

CLOTILDE, *pointing.* Look! There!... Someone's coming...

HERMIONE. Who?

VÉNUS. It's Timur...

CLOTILDE. Oh my!... He's talking to Juan...

VÉNUS. He's beating him!

HERMIONE. With his hatchet... He'll kill him! He'll—

CLOTILDE. Look at his skull! Oh...

The three gasp in horror and disbelief.

VÉNUS. Here they come...

> TIMUR *and* ALMANZOR *enter, right, followed by* HÉLÈNE, *who hangs back, and the several blacks.*

CÉLESTINE. So many people! Papá will be pleased! His blacks are so happy...

TIMUR, *brandishing his bloody hatchet.* And if anyone has any complaints, let him step forward!

MARIE-LOUISE, *to* CÉLESTINE. My child...

> *The blacks mumble their disapproval.*

JEAN-JACQUES, *stepping forward.* I will, Timur!

ALMANZOR. So will I! It's too much! *(To* TIMUR.*)* You... Why did you split Juan's skull? Why did you have to kill him?

TIMUR. Why, you ask? I leave you to guard three prisoners. And what do I find? One of them being whipped! And when I cry out, Juan stabs him, dead! That is why! *(Brandishing his hatchet.)* To teach him to disobey!

JEAN-JACQUES. Disobey?

The other blacks echo: "Disobey, disobey?"

ALMANZOR, *to* TIMUR. Have you turned white... *(sarcastically)...* master?

TÉLÉMAQUE. I liked Morin better!

JEAN-JACQUES, *to* TIMUR. We're tired of your orders! (*Pointing to* LÉON *and* CÉLESTINE.) And those two? The ones you want us to keep guarding forever?

TIMUR. So?

JEAN-JACQUES. We want to be rid of them! We want our revenge!

TIMUR. Why the hurry, my friend? What did they ever do to you? Only treated you well... Oh, no field work for the likes of you! You who lived in their house, who ate their food... In return for a few simple chores...

JEAN-JACQUES. Simple chores...

ALMANZOR. A few...

TIMUR, *to* JEAN-JACQUES. Mad dog, you! Or worse! You can't wait to rip your master to shreds! And me, his enemy... The one that he wronged... I am taking my time, and I refuse to be hurried.

JEAN-JACQUES. Say what you like. We want our revenge! Slit his throat if that's your pleasure. Slice open his belly. Smash both his arms to bits. Whatever suits your fancy, Timur. But do something! Show no mercy...

TIMUR. No mercy? *(With a sardonic little laugh.)* At times I might almost have been tempted... But no...

ALMANZOR. Look here, Timur. You didn't think twice about splitting poor Juan's skull! What are you waiting for? Be quick!

JEAN-JACQUES. Finish the job!

ALMANZOR. Jean-Pierre would never have made us wait this long...

TIMUR. Jean-Pierre?... If you love Jean-Pierre so much, why not go get him? Find him and bring him back!

ALMANZOR. Why not? I will...

JEAN-JACQUES. We both will...

ALMANZOR. At least he's a good black! A real one... Not like—

> *The blacks echo with shouts of "A real black...," "Jean-Pierre...," "He is, he is...," etc.*

TIMUR, *to himself.* Bah! Let them go... *(To the blacks.)* Listen, all of you... My brothers... Do you really want those two whites to die? Do you hate them so little? Would you spare them their suffering? Tell me, did the whites kill us all at once? How long did they make us die by degrees? How many days? How many hours? How long did each one of us spend rotting in the hold? In the jail? In the fields? Working in the presses?... I died here every minute for four whole years! And you want me to kill them just like that? All at once? Like that poor negress... Remember?... The one they gave a hundred lashes, so we killed her with a pick-axe to put her out of her misery!... Is that what you want?... No, no... They don't deserve it. They have to wait, to suffer...

JEAN-JACQUES. What is he saying?

TIMUR, *continuing.* They have to spend a long time dying. Really, my brothers! What change has come over you? Do you pity them that much?

TÉLÉMAQUE, *nodding.* I know what he means. It's true, what he says...

ALMANZOR, *to* TIMUR. Do as you like then. Kill them slowly if you wish. Only kill them! I want to see their blood! Their blood, you hear?

> *The blacks mutter their approval: "Their blood, their blood!"*
> *"We want to see it!" etc.*

TIMUR. Patience, patience!... Do you think I thirst for it any less than you? More! Even more! But all in good time. I am free now, and I must do as I see fit. I cannot let you all become the masters.

JEAN-JACQUES. But...

ALMANZOR. Timur...

TIMUR. Enough!... I am either free or I am not... Now, all of you... *(With a sweeping gesture.)* Leave! I have to be by myself... I have things to do.

ALMANZOR. But the two whites—

TIMUR. I told you. I shall have my revenge! You think I do not hate them? Go, I told you! I have to be alone.

ALMANZOR. Good! Do as you like. But we are going to find Jean-Pierre, Timur. You understand? And we'll see when we come back!

JEAN-JACQUES. Yes. We'll see if you have avenged us.

TIMUR. You'll see... *(To* ALMANZOR.*)* You'll see...

JEAN-JACQUES, *approaching* LÉON. Ah, master! *Au revoir... (Sarcastically.)* I'll lay monsieur's clothes out... *(emphasizing)* ...Master!

LÉON. Swine!

JEAN-JACQUES. For the last time... Master!

TIMUR, *to* ALMANZOR *and* JEAN-JACQUES. Will you leave!

ALMANZOR. We're going...

JEAN-JACQUES, *to the other blacks, softly.* He wants to betray you... To betray us all...

ALMANZOR, *softly.* We'll find Jean-Pierre and tell him.

MARIE-LOUISE, *to* TIMUR, *throwing herself at his feet.* Ah, Timur! Please!... I beg you! Spare mademoiselle... My child, my daughter...

TIMUR. Your daughter?... Then woe to the hen who hatches the serpent's eggs! (*To* JEAN-JACQUES.) Get this old she-ape out of my sight!

JEAN-JACQUES. With pleasure...

> *He seizes her and drags her off, left.* ALMANZOR *follows close behind.*

TIMUR, *to* HÉLÈNE, *still hanging back, down right.* You! (*Coldly.*) Go with the women!

HÉLÈNE. Oh, Touko! (*Weeping.*) I'm afraid...

TIMUR. Go, I said! I have no need for you here.

HÉLÈNE. But my love...

TIMUR, *sharply, pointing left.* Out! (*To* VÉNUS.) Take her away.

VÉNUS, *to* HÉLÈNE. Come... You can cry your eyes out...

> *She pulls her, struggling, left to join the women, as* ALMAN-ZOR, JEAN-JACQUES, *and* TÉLÉMAQUE *exit, left. The remaining blacks disperse in every direction, leaving* TIMUR *alone with* CÉLESTINE *and* LÉON.

TIMUR. At last... Alone... And free... *(Coming down right, musing.)* How impossible, to be free as long as there is someone else... But now, I am. *(Looking at* LÉON *and* CÉLESTINE.*)* Except for them... Except for my prey... And now I can devour it, just as I please! Finally, I can be happy! I can do... *(hesitating)* ...what I want to do!... Yes, what *I* want... Myself... *(Looking off, left.)* Not those insolent scoundrels!... Ah! Strange, how much colder my revenge seems now... Now that they try to force me... *(Recovering his aplomb.)* No! Nonsense, Timur! You're mad! Revenge is revenge, and I swore it! I swore... Come now, be a man! The banana trees, Timur... Remember? *(He approaches* LÉON.*)* Him! And the banana trees... Ah yes, my revenge... *(To* LÉON.*)* So? Monsieur? *(Scornfully.)* Master?... Nothing to say, Léon? Nothing to tell each other, you and I? *(*LÉON *shakes his head.)* You heard their demands? You heard what I promised?

LÉON, *weakly.* No matter... I only want to die... Nothing else...

TIMUR. Ah yes...

LÉON. But at your hands, not theirs... Not those wild, foul beasts... At least you have the right to hate me...

TIMUR. Oh yes, Léon! I have the right! And I hate more than you know. And you will die, I promise!

LÉON. Then strike, Timur! It's time! Only one thing I beg you... I beseech you, Timur... My sister has done nothing to earn your hate. Please... Mercy... Spare her life!

TIMUR. Your sister?... Yes, I feel no hatred for her. You need not be concerned. *(With a sardonic smile.)* Oh yes, she will go free.

LÉON. Then kill me and be done with it. The poor thing will never know...

TIMUR. Be done with it, you say? What? So soon? You think you deserve such an easy death? Your father, yes... What did he do, after all?.... But you, Léon? Ah! *(Sarcastically.)* You deserve better! *(To* CÉLESTINE.) Come, you... White woman!

LÉON, *suspecting his intent.* What? What are you saying? Please... Tell me...

TIMUR. Ah, Léon... Léon! The banana trees? You remember?

LÉON. Only too well! I would rather die than think about them.

TIMUR. Ah yes... So would I! If only I might have... But you preferred to torture me! You preferred to fill me with rage and despair!

LÉON. Timur...

TIMUR. Well, what you preferred, I prefer too. Yes! Suffer what I suffered! Yes, Léon! Watch your sister! Watch *us!* Watch *us!*

LÉON, *realizing his intent.* Good God! No! You wouldn't... Oh, barbarian! You beast! A poor, innocent child... And out of her mind... Oh, mercy! Mercy!

TIMUR. And did you show mercy, on the ground, by the banana trees? Mercy! Ha! *(To* CÉLESTINE.) Come, white woman! *(He cuts her cords with his hatchet.)* You are free!

CÉLESTINE. Oh, the pretty black!

LÉON. God above!

CÉLESTINE. What game shall we play?

LÉON, *to* TIMUR. You monster! How can you... Don't touch her!

TIMUR. Quiet! This slave is mine!

As he is about to drag her off, HÉLÈNE *comes running in, left, and throws herself between them.*

HÉLÈNE. Touko!

TIMUR. Badia!

HÉLÈNE. What are you doing? You... With her...

LÉON. Hélène... Stop him... Don't let him—

HÉLÈNE, *to* TIMUR, *pointing.* His sister... His... The white devil's sister...

TIMUR. But...

HÉLÈNE. No, Touko! Choose! You must! You must!

TIMUR, *to himself.* Oh! What was I thinking... How could I... (*To* HÉLÈNE.) Badia... My Badia... Please...

> *He lets go of* CÉLESTINE *and takes* HÉLÈNE *in his arms, kissing her.*

CÉLESTINE. Oh, black man! Kiss me too!

TIMUR, *to* HÉLÈNE. Can you forgive me?

LÉON, *heaving a sigh.* Thank God!

HÉLÈNE. Touko, dearest! We have no time... They're coming to get you! Your life is in danger!

TIMUR. My life?

HÉLÈNE. Just now, when I left... (*Pointing left.*) I followed behind them. I listened to them talking. When they found Jean-Pierre they told him about Juan, and how you killed him. And he flew into a rage, Touko. He swore he would make you pay with your life. He says you're a traitor, and he's arming them all... (*Pointing to* LÉON.) He says that, if they find that one alive, they should kill you!

TIMUR. Oh? Kill me, will they? Do they think I fear their threats? Do they think they are the masters? Do they think I am their slave?

HÉLÈNE. Touko...

TIMUR. Kill me?... Well, we shall see how they kill me! *(To* LÉON, *cutting his bonds.)* Live, white man! Let them find you alive! Yes, let them find you! Alive and free!

LÉON. What?

TIMUR. So be it!

LÉON. Just when...

TIMUR. We shall see who is the master!

LÉON. I... I don't understand...

TIMUR. Have no fear, white dog!

LÉON. But...

TIMUR. Oh yes, I hate you! I loathe you still. But your life is sacred to me now... You, my proof against them!... I have had my revenge!

HÉLÈNE. Touko?

TIMUR, *to* LÉON. I shall defend you if I must!

LÉON. And I hate you no less, Timur. But I shall defend you as well. Count on me!

TIMUR, *shaking his hand.* Count on me!

CÉLESTINE, *looking on.* Come, brother dear. We have been waiting for you. Papá is wondering what is taking you so long.

LÉON, *shaking his head.* Alas!

TIMUR, *looking right, off in the distance.* They are coming... I need your help, Léon. More is at stake than my life and yours. The blacks will be doomed. They are lost without me... *(With a gesture upstage.)* Follow me...

He takes HÉLÈNE *by the hand and leads her up the hill.*

LÉON. Yes... Up the hill... We can save ourselves if we must... (*To* CÉLESTINE.) Come, sister dear...

They follow TIMUR.

TIMUR. I see them!... (*To* LÉON.) Here! (*Taking a dagger from his belt, he gives it to* LÉON.) Take this...

> *As he and* HÉLÈNE *crouch out of sight, the blacks, men and women, enter, right, milling about.* ALMANZOR, JEAN-PIERRE, JEAN-JACQUES, TÉLÉMAQUE, CLOTILDE, VÉNUS, *and* HERMIONE *are among them.*

ALMANZOR, *looking about.* Where are they? I was sure—

JEAN-PIERRE. So, brothers?

ALMANZOR. Treason! They've run off!

> TIMUR *stands up, tall, atop the hill, leaving* HÉLÈNE *concealed.*

JEAN-JACQUES. Not at all, Zozor... (*Pointing to* TIMUR.) There!... Timur, we have returned.

TIMUR. So I see. And what do you wish?

> *He comes down the hill and stands boldly in front of the others.*

JEAN-JACQUES. You know what we wish!

JEAN-PIERRE. The white man's death or yours!

TIMUR. The white man's death? And by what right? I take my vengeance as I see fit!

ALMANZOR. Oh?

TIMUR. My hatred has been fulfilled. As long as I am satisfied, you can all hold your tongues!

JEAN-PIERRE. But we...

JEAN-JACQUES. But Timur...

TIMUR. Hold your tongues, I said! There is nothing here for you. *(Pointing to* LÉON.) And woe unto anyone who touches a single hair of that man's head!

JEAN-JACQUES. *His* head, Timur?

JEAN-PIERRE. *His* head?

ALMANZOR, *to* TIMUR. And yours? What about yours?

JEAN-PIERRE, *to* TIMUR. Yes! Your traitor's head!

TIMUR. You want my head? Come take it, Jean-Pierre! Or you, Jean-Jacques?... *(He holds out his hatchet and stands waiting for a long moment.)* You, Almanzor?... Well? I'm waiting!... What? No one?... Not one of you?... Cowards, one and all! Cowards! Like the other night, when I called on you to rise up! To revolt against your masters...

ALMANZOR. But Timur...

The blacks, grumbling, mutter their disagreement.

TIMUR. Ah yes... Just the same... And now that you are free you are not one whit better! Still cowards, you hear? *(Shouting.)* Cowards!... Well, kill me then if you dare! And when the whites come back... When they invade...

JEAN-JACQUES. What? The whites?

TIMUR, *continuing.* We shall see just what you can do!

ALMANZOR, *to* JEAN-PIERRE. Did he say "the whites"?

TÉLÉMAQUE. Ay ay ay!

JEAN-PIERRE. Don't listen! He doesn't know—

ALMANZOR. The whites? Invade...?

TIMUR. Why should you be afraid, my friends? Will you not have
my head to present them? A gift like that should earn you their
mercy! No, they will not harm you... As long as all of you, qui-
etly and calmly, hack up the earth once more, and pile the sugarcane in the carts... As long as each one of you, without a murmur, accepts your daily ration of the whip, and a score of you let
them put you in chains, and five or six get torn limb from limb or
hanged... And you, Jean-Pierre... Yes, perhaps only you will be
buried alive. But outside of that... No, the whites will not harm
you. Why should they, when you bring them the head of Timur?

ALMANZOR, *to* JEAN-PIERRE. You hear that?

TÉLÉMAQUE. God, if it's true...

JEAN-PIERRE, *shaken.* Buried alive?

JEAN-JACQUES. You never told us that, Jean-Pierre!

JEAN-PIERRE. But... I... I didn't know...

ALMANZOR. But that's what he said...

JEAN-JACQUES, *to* TIMUR. Look, Timur... No one here has anything
against you. And everyone knows how intelligent you are, and
what a good leader... But that white villain... No! We want him
dead, that's all. A little swing of your hatchet and we'll all be
happy! Why not—

TIMUR, *interrupting, angrily.* Enough, I told you! He lives or we both die! Is that clear? That is all I have to say.

JEAN-JACQUES. Damnation! How much more...

> *He cocks his rifle, takes aim at* LÉON, *and fires. The bullet hits* CÉLESTINE, *whom* LÉON *is still clutching to his breast.*

CÉLESTINE. Oh... The pain...

LÉON. Célestine!... *(She writhes for a moment and falls dead at his feet.)* No! No!... *(Lifting her in his arms.)* Sister dear... *(Shaking his head.)* God help us! *(Looking about in utter despair.)* Nothing... Nothing... *(To* TIMUR.) Live, Timur! Live your life... And be the master!

TIMUR. Monsieur...

LÉON. Adieu, Timur!

> *Suddenly, still clutching* CÉLESTINE*'s lifeless body, he turns and flings himself off the hill and into the sea. As* TIMUR, *gasping, takes a few steps up the hill, looking out over the water, the blacks raise spontaneous cries of "Hurrah!" "He's dead!" "At last!" etc.*

TIMUR. Oh... *(Shaking his head.)* Gone... *(Angrily.)* Why? Why, I ask you... *(Apostrophizing.)* You poor, wretched souls! You deserved a better end! *(To the blacks, as they continue their joyous shouts in counterpoint to his anger.)* He did... They did... That white was a good man... A good man, I tell you... *(Coming down center, to* JEAN-PIERRE.) So! You still want my head?

JEAN-PIERRE. Why not, you traitor? You didn't kill him, did you?

JEAN-JACQUES, *to* TIMUR, *sarcastically.* That good white of yours!

The blacks echo their angry accusations: "That good white man!" "You traitor!" "You didn't kill him, Timur!" etc. As they are about to turn on him, a black comes running in, right, excited and breathless, almost collapsing, center stage.

ALMANZOR, *sensing trouble.* Wait!... (*To* THE BLACK.) What is it?

JEAN-PIERRE. What?

JEAN-JACQUES. Tell us!

THE BLACK. Them... They're coming...

JEAN-JACQUES. Who?

THE BLACK. The whites... They're coming...

TIMUR. The whites! You see?

THE BLACK. To take us back!

There is general consternation and shock. Everyone, in panic, begins shouting: "The whites! The whites!"

ALMANZOR. To take us back?

TÉLÉMAQUE. Or to kill us!

THE BLACK. From the militia... All of them... With their guns...

JEAN-JACQUES *drops his rifle in panic and runs off, left.* JEAN-PIERRE *and* ALMANZOR *follow him, with* TÉLÉMAQUE *loping after them. One can hear a number of shots coming from off right, and the sounds of men approaching. Several blacks, ostensibly escaping from the oncoming whites, come running in, right.*

TIMUR, *shouting to make himself heard above the confusion.* Come, all of you! Come!

HÉLÈNE, *running down from the hill and joining him.* Save us, Touko!

> *Everyone calls out to him: "Save us, Timur!" "Only you can save us!" "Only you! Only you!" etc.*

TIMUR. Are you with me? *(They all reply: "We are! We are!")* Then follow me, Africans!... Obey, my children! Obey, and you shall be free!

> *He leads them off, left. The sound of gunshots and the approaching whites grows louder. In the distance the ruins continue to smolder against the brightening sky.*

CURTAIN